OLIVER PLUNKETT
IN HIS OWN WORDS

Desmond Forristal

OLIVER PLUNKETT
IN HIS OWN WORDS

VERITAS

First published 1975 by
Veritas Publications
This edition published 2001 by
Veritas Publications
7/8 Lower Abbey Street
Dublin 1

Nihil Obstat:
Kevin Kennedy, D.D.

Imprimi potest:
✠ Dermot
Archbishop of Dublin,
18 April 1975

The nihil obstat *and* imprimatur *are a declaration that a text is considered to be free of doctrinal or moral error. They do not necessarily imply agreement with opinions expressed by the author.*

ISBN 1 85390 567 4

British Library Cataloguing
in Publication Data.
A catalogue record for
this book is available
from the British Library.

Cover design by Bill Bolger
Printed in the Republic of Ireland by Betaprint Ltd, Dublin

Veritas books are printed on paper made from the wood pulp of managed forests. For every tree felled, at least one tree is planted, thereby renewing natural resources.

CONTENTS

1

In His Own Words

About Oliver Plunkett we have a great mass of information, yet we sometimes feel we hardly know the man at all. The events of his life are recorded in minute detail in the writings of his time but the personality of the man behind the events remains frustratingly elusive.

The reason is simple enough. Nearly all our information about Oliver comes from official sources, from reports, state papers, legal records, Church documents. They give us many facts but little enough of the human background to the facts. In all the countless references to the Archbishop there is not one that gives us a description of his physical appearance, his voice, his accent, his manner of speaking or of moving, or any of the other personal traits and mannerisms that must have been so obvious to his contemporaries but are hidden from later generations.

Neither do we have anything like a convincing character-sketch from any of those who knew him. There is praise and blame of him in plenty, but the one must be regarded with as much caution as the other. Much of the praise is of a conventional sort, especially that written after his death when he was already beginning to take on the aura of a martyr and the writers seemed more concerned with edifying their readers than recording their exact impressions. There is the same lack of reality about the adverse opinions, which generally show obvious malice and are aimed at justifying the writer for his part in some long forgotten dispute with the Archbishop. It is only occasionally that one comes across an impression or an incident that seems to suggest a real man with the good and bad qualities of a real man and not a stylised saint or villain.

To paint his portrait, this book relies mainly upon the man's own words. Fortunately, Oliver Plunkett was an indefatigable letter-writer and, equally fortunately, many of these letters have been preserved.

During his active years as Archbishop of Armagh he corresponded continually with the Vatican, reporting on all his activities and on the state of the Irish Church. These letters, still preserved in the Roman archives, are the main source of our information about him and about the Catholic Church in Ireland in the 1670s.

Yet here again we are doomed to disappointment if we expect any intimate personal revelations, for this was an official correspondence. It was the area representative reporting back to head office, and the facts and figures were what mattered, not the feelings of the writer. No one wears his heart upon his sleeve when writing to an official he may never even have met. In addition, Oliver was inhibited by the suspicion that his letters were being opened and read by Dublin Castle on their way to Rome, a suspicion that later proved to be only too well founded. Nevertheless, between the lines we get an occasional glimpse of the personality of the writer, all the more authentic in that it is unwittingly given us.

One small group of letters falls into a category of its own. These are the letters that he wrote in his prison cell during the two weeks before his death. Two of these were written to a young kinsman in Rome, the remainder to a Benedictine monk who was his fellow-prisoner in Newgate. In these letters, for the first and only time that we know of, he opened his mind and heart fully in writing to another person. From these faded documents, through their quaint old-fashioned language, there comes to us across a gap of three centuries the truest picture we have of Oliver Plunkett, written in his own words.

2

BOYHOOD AND PRIESTHOOD

Oliver Plunkett was born on 1 November 1625 at Loughcrew, near Oldcastle in County Meath. His father was John Plunkett, Baron of Loughcrew, and his mother was born Thomasina Dillon, grand-daughter of Sir Luke Dillon. Oliver came of an aristocratic family in an age when aristocracy meant not just prestige but power and wealth. In Ireland as in every other country of Europe there was a sharp dividing line between the great mass of the people, the peasants and the artisans, and the few noble families who kept all the reins of influence in their small circle and who married their sons and daughters to one another until everybody was related to everybody else. A testimonial letter from the Rector of the Irish College in Rome described Oliver as being 'of Catholic parentage, descended from an illustrious family: on the father's side from the most illustrious Earls of Fingal and on the mother's side from the most illustrious Earls of Roscommon, and also connected by birth with the most illustrious Oliver Plunkett, Baron of Louth, first Nobleman of the Diocese of Armagh'; and the information was obviously provided by Oliver himself. He might have come from an obscure corner of an obscure land but the blood of noble forebears flowed in his veins. He was human enough to take pride in the fact and wise enough to take advantage of it for a good cause.

Oliver was one of a family of five, with an elder brother, Edward, and three younger sisters, Catherine, Anne and Mary. His boyhood was an untroubled one: it was a relatively peaceful period in Ireland and the laws against Catholics were not rigidly enforced. In any event, Oliver's family connections protected him against both religious discrimination and the poverty that gripped the vast majority of his fellow-countrymen. They also solved the problem of his education, and his parents naturally thought of Dr Patrick Plunkett, a first cousin of Oliver's mother, when the question of his schooling came up.

Patrick Plunkett was the first great formative influence on Oliver's life and he supervised the boy's education from childhood until his sixteenth year. When he first received the youngster into his household, Patrick was aged about thirty and was acting parish priest in Kilcloon in County Meath. A few years later he was appointed Abbot of St Mary's in Dublin, and later still was to be Bishop successively of Ardagh and of Meath. We have no record of the course of studies that Oliver followed under his guidance but it is clear that the older man made a profound impression on his young pupil. In after years, Oliver always spoke of him with great respect and affection.

It was on Patrick Plunkett's advice that Oliver decided to go to Rome to study for the priesthood. In 1641 the Ulster rebellion put an end to the peace of the country and to Oliver's education. The movement, which sparked off in Ulster, spread rapidly and led, the following year, to the formation of the Confederation of Kilkenny, a kind of parliament that had the support not only of the native Irish but of the Anglo-Irish gentry as well. Among the Plunketts who made their way to Kilkenny was Patrick, taking his place among the Lords Spiritual in the new parliament. It was evident that he could no longer continue as Oliver's tutor and anyhow the boy had now reached the stage where he needed a more formal and structured education. The war-torn Ireland of the 1640s could not offer such an education. The Irish College in Rome could.

About Oliver's reasons for choosing the priesthood we know little. The staunch faith of his own parents and home must certainly have been one factor, the example of Patrick Plunkett another, and perhaps a more powerful one. As the younger son, he had no rights or responsibilities in regard to the family estates, and the choice of his career was left to his own judgment. He chose the priesthood, and having made his choice he followed it with the tenacity and singleness of purpose that were to be so characteristic of him in later life. Obstacles existed only in order to be overcome.

The obstacles that lay between Oliver and Rome were forbidding enough. Even in peacetime, a journey to Rome was a formidable undertaking. Ships often waited weeks in port for a favourable wind, and even when at last sea-borne, had to run the danger of both storms and pirates. Land travel was almost as uncertain, with muddy roads, flooded rivers, and bandits lurking in every wood and mountain valley. To these normal hazards, there was now the added complication of war. Ireland was an armed camp, England was a battlefield between Royalists and Puritans, Northern Europe was still in the grip of the Thirty Years War.

It was not until 1646 that an opportunity presented itself. Father Peter Scarampi had been sent by the Pope as an envoy to the Confederation of Kilkenny. Towards the end of 1646, his mission accomplished, he was returning to Rome and had chartered a ship from Waterford. He offered to take with him some students for the Irish College and a group of five suitable young men was assembled in Waterford in December of that year. Oliver Plunkett was one of them. Another was John Brennan, later Archbishop of Cashel, who was to become Oliver's constant companion and closest friend to the end of his life.

As usually happened with Oliver, the winds proved unfavourable. It was not until 12 February 1647 that the ship could leave Waterford. The dangers from pirates and storms still remained to be faced and both duly made their appearance; fortunately for the travellers, they appeared at the same time. On the morning of the second day they spied two larger vessels bearing down on them with hostile intent. The sailors crowded on every stitch of canvas but it soon became clear that the enemy ships were gaining on them, and by nightfall they were only a short distance away.

Father Scarampi and his young companions joined in prayer for deliverance from their pursuers and promised to go in pilgrimage to the shrine of Saint Francis of Assisi if they escaped. During the night a violent storm blew up and continued for the following two days. The ship was tossed around by mountainous seas and the young men making their first voyage must have longed to feel the firm ground of Ireland beneath their feet again. On the third day, however, the storm blew itself out, the wind died down, and the sea calmed. The ship had been blown many miles off its course but the two enemy vessels had disappeared and were not sighted again for the remainder of the voyage.

On 4 March they landed at Ostend and set out for Paris. Their troubles were not yet over. In Flanders they fell into the hands of a band of robbers who took all their valuables and held them to ransom. Somehow or other, the ransom was paid and the travellers resumed their journey. Passing through Paris and Lyons, they entered Italy and made first for Assisi to fulfil their promise to Saint Francis. It was well into the month of May when they finally entered Rome. The journey from Ireland had taken three months; if one takes into account the delay in Waterford, five months.

Like many an Irishman before him and after him, Oliver grew to love Rome and feel very much at home there. After the turmoil of his native country, the peace and order of the city were all the more striking to the young man. The contrast between the splendour of the Church in Rome and its poverty in Ireland was especially noticeable. In the recently completed Basilica of Saint Peter's, the Pope presided over the solemn ceremonies in golden vestments. The finest painters, sculptors, and composers of the day were employed to give great magnificence to the liturgy. Bernini, greatest of all baroque architects, was at the height of his powers and new churches designed by him and his disciples were adding new glory to the city. To wander through the streets of Rome, to visit the Colosseum and the catacombs, to watch the old buildings being demolished and the new ones taking their place, merely to stand and see people of many nationalities passing by, was a heady experience for the young Irishman and one that he never forgot.

The news that continued to come from Ireland during Oliver's student days made the difference between the two countries more cruelly apparent than ever. By 1649 the Confederation of Kilkenny had broken up in disorder and Cromwell and his army had landed in Ireland to mop up what resistance still remained. His first and most spectacular act of vengeance was against the city of Drogheda, on the border of Oliver's native county. The entire garrison of more than two thousand men were put to the sword and when some of the defenders took refuge in Saint Peter's Church, Cromwell ordered that the building be burnt around them. Many civilians died, and priests and friars were hunted down with particular ferocity. It was, wrote Cromwell, a 'righteous judgment of God upon these barbarous wretches, who have imbrued their hands in so much innocent blood'. During the years that followed, Cromwell and his lieutenants continued to wreak God's righteous judgment upon the barbarous Irish. One after another, the Irish towns fell to the invaders, the last in 1652. Everywhere churches were burnt, monasteries scattered, bishops and priests killed or exiled or imprisoned.

What the sword began, the law completed. The final stage in Cromwell's plan was the replacing of Irish Catholics by English Protestants. The natives were to lose all their lands in Munster, Leinster and Ulster and remove themselves to the inhospitable wastes of Connaught. Among those who lost all their property was Oliver's elder brother, who had succeeded to the estate on the death of their father. By the end of 1653 Cromwell felt that he had at last found the final solution to the Irish problem.

On 1 January 1654 Oliver Plunkett was ordained priest in Rome. He had been an excellent student, intelligent, studious and devout; the rector of the Irish College later described him as 'a model of gentleness, integrity and piety'. Now, in accordance with the vow taken by all students of the College, he was to return to Ireland. It was not a cheering prospect, and on 14 June he wrote to the Jesuit General asking to be dispensed from his vow. The letter was written in Latin and is the earliest of his writings still preserved for us.

> I, Oliver Plunkett, your most humble petitioner, student of the Irish College, having completed my philosophical and theological studies, in view of the impossibility (well known to your Paternity) of my now returning to Ireland as demanded by the rules of the College and the oath I have taken, do humbly request of you, Most Reverend Father, that I may be allowed to remain in Rome and reside with the Fathers of San Girolamo della Carità. I promise, however, and declare that I will be always ready to return to Ireland whenever you, Reverend Father, or my superiors shall so command.

No doubt Oliver was only following standard practice in writing this request: his friend, John Brennan, also remained in Rome and there is no evidence that any of his fellow-students returned home at this period. No doubt too, his chances of getting safely into Ireland were slight: the ports were watched and there were spies everywhere. Yet one would like to feel certain that Oliver made his request only with reluctance, that it took days and perhaps weeks of argument on the part of friends and superiors to convince him that his duty lay in Rome and not among his own people. It would certainly have been difficult for him to return to Ireland but it would not have been impossible. But to a young man of Oliver's ability Rome offered an attractive and honourable career while Ireland held out only the prospect of imprisonment and death.

In these circumstances it was easy enough for him to decide that the prudent course and the course most agreeable to God's will was for him to stay in Rome. He may have been right in that decision but he can hardly have been particularly proud of it. In the years that followed he may have wondered how much fear mingled with the prudence and how he would bear himself if ever called upon to choose between his life and his principles. It was not until his last days on earth that these doubts were to be finally laid to rest.

Meanwhile, Oliver's ecclesiastical career proceeded smoothly on its course. He continued his studies, attending the lectures on Canon and Civil Law given by Mariscotti, and in due course obtained his doctorate in these two subjects. In 1657 he was appointed Professor of Theology in Propaganda College and was later appointed a Consultor of the Congregation of the Index. He also became active as the agent of the Irish clergy in their dealings with the Vatican. The death of Cromwell in 1658 and the restoration of King Charles II had brought about an easing of the situation in Ireland. The clergy found Oliver always ready to use his influence with the Roman Congregations on behalf of his Irish friends.

Of his private life during the same period less is known. Writing after Oliver's death and when he had already begun to take on the martyr's aura, the Italian writer Marangoni described his life at San Girolamo in these words:

> Here it is incredible with what zeal he burned for the salvation of souls. In the house itself and in the city he wholly devoted himself to devout exercises; frequently did he visit the

sanctuaries steeped with the blood of so many martyrs and he ardently sighed for the opportunity of sacrificing himself for the salvation of his countrymen. He moreover frequented the hospital of Santo Spirito and employed himself even in the most abject ministrations, serving the sick poor to the edification and wonder of the very officials and assistants of that place.

This is Italian hagiography at its most voluptuous. The picture of Oliver sighing ardently around the tombs of the martyrs in his desire to die for his countrymen is hard to take seriously, especially when we remember the efforts he had recently been making to avoid doing precisely that. Yet Marangoni was a reputable historian and beneath the verbiage there must be a foundation of truth. Perhaps Oliver was still troubled by his decision to opt for the peace of Rome, still uneasily aware that men were fighting and suffering in the front line while he pushed a pen at staff headquarters.

It may have been partly a desire to share in the hardships of the active troops that led Oliver to undertake spare-time work in the hospitals. This part of Marangoni's description is corroborated by a letter of Oliver's in which he speaks of his friend Monsignor Odescalchi, who later became Pope Innocent XI. 'I often assisted him when he tended the poor and ragged and needy, many of them covered with vermin. He gave them shelter and clothing at his own expense, he washed and fed them with his own hands.' It is an unexpected occupation for the Professor of Theology and second son of the Baron of Loughcrew, and it shows a side of Oliver's character that we have not seen before.

3

THE NEW ARCHBISHOP

At the beginning of the year 1669 there was only one Catholic bishop active in Ireland, none other than Oliver's durable kinsman, Patrick Plunkett, who that year was transferred from Ardagh to the more prosperous diocese of Meath. The only other bishop in the country was an invalid, the Bishop of Kilmore, 'continually infirm in body and occasionally in mind' according to Bishop Plunkett. Three others, including the Archbishop of Armagh, Edmund O'Reilly, were living in exile. The Church in Ireland was recovering from the Cromwellian persecution but recovery was bringing its own problems. The clergy were divided into several quarrelling factions and the lack of a resident hierarchy made it difficult to settle these disputes and restore ecclesiastical discipline.

Accordingly, the Roman authorities decided to appoint new bishops to a number of vacant sees. Dr Peter Talbot, a close friend of the reigning monarch, Charles II, was appointed Archbishop of Dublin. New archbishops were also appointed to Tuam and Cashel and a new bishop to Ossory. Then news arrived in Rome that the Archbishop of Armagh had died in France, leaving vacant the most important see in Ireland. The choice of his successor would obviously be of crucial importance to the future of the Irish Church.

Immediately the lobbying began. The new Archbishop of Dublin sent in a list of three names and added some unkind remarks about the clergy of Armagh. The clergy of Armagh did nothing to improve their image by writing to threaten uproar if an outsider and particularly a Meath man were appointed to their diocese. Oliver himself, the most obvious candidate for the position, at first let it be known that he wished to remain on in Rome and complete some books he was working on. Later he changed his mind or was persuaded to change his mind and formally put forward his name.

The meeting of the Congregation of Propaganda that was to make the appointment was held on 9 July. The Pope himself, Clement IX, was present. After an indecisive discussion about the names proposed by Dr Talbot, all of whom were unsuitable for one reason or another, the Pope impatiently cut short the proceedings. It was a waste of time, he said, to talk about candidates of doubtful suitability when they had in Rome a man who was certainly fitted in every way for the position. That man was Oliver Plunkett.

The announcement of his appointment was greeted with a chorus of praise, led by Archbishop Talbot. Only the clergy of Armagh remained silent, stunned by the imposition of a Meath man upon their diocese. Meanwhile preparations were put in hand for the consecration of the new Primate. The Roman authorities thought it unwise to provoke the English government by too much publicly; so it was decided that Oliver should leave Rome quietly for Belgium, where he would be consecrated in a private ceremony, and from there make his way to Ireland.

Before leaving Rome, Oliver paid a last visit to the Hospital of Santo Spirito. Father Miesknow, the Superior, said to him: 'Monsignor, you are now going to shed your blood for the Catholic faith.' The Archbishop-elect answered: 'I am not worthy of that; but pray for me that my desire for it may be fulfilled.' The story comes from Marangoni, who relates it with the customary embellishments: but as he adds the name of an eye-witness, it is probably substantially true.

Before he had even set foot in Ireland, the new Archbishop had begun the long series of reports and letters to Rome that give us so much information about his activities during the next ten years. His journey to Belgium had been comparatively uneventful and his consecration had taken place according to plan in the private chapel of the Bishop of Ghent, on 1 December. He then made his way to London and from there wrote on the thirtieth of that month to Cardinal Barberini in Rome. The Queen he refers to is Catherine of Braganza, wife of Charles II, who was a Catholic and was allowed by the terms of her marriage treaty to maintain a chapel and priest to serve in it.

I presented Your Eminence's letters to the Queen, who gave me a very gracious audience and spoke highly of you for the affection you have always shown for her and the King and entire nation. She added that those sent by you have always been well-disposed to His Majesty and she hoped for the same from me. I spoke with some of the King's intimates and they told me that he often refers to Your Eminence with affection and regard.

I also delivered your letter to Father Howard, and Grand Almoner, a truly worthy man. He secretly let me stay with him for ten days in his own apartments in the Royal Palace. He also very kindly brought me out driving on several occasions in his carriage to see the principal sights of the city. . . .

It is so cold here at the moment that the Spanish wine actually froze in my chalice. They have not had as bad a winter as this for many years. After the frost there was a heavy fall of snow so that it will be morally impossible to travel until the cold spell is over.

I am not at all anxious, however, to stay on in London in view of the attitude of the Court. The followers of Walsh, or more likely Walsh himself, keep sending anonymous letters to the Ministers of Court, filled with lying stories about what I am doing here; but their ill-will is well known and they themselves are regarded with contempt. One letter to the King said that Father Howard had three hundred priests hidden in the Royal Palace who went around every night trying to make converts for the Pope. One good thing about these stories is they are so far-fetched that no one believes their authors even when they happen to tell the truth.

It was not until March that Oliver arrived in Ireland, after an absence of twenty-three years. The journey from Rome to Dublin had taken nearly seven months of weary winter travel but the warmth of the welcome that greeted him atoned for a lot. Various noble Plunketts hastened to congratulate the Archbishop on this new honour to their family. Among those he was most glad to see were

Bishop Patrick Plunkett, his old friend, and the Bishop's brother, Sir
Nicholas Plunkett. He wrote to Rome to report his arrival.

> I arrived in this city at long last on Monday. I can say that I
> suffered more on the journey from London to Holyhead,
> where I took the boat, than on all the journey from Rome to
> London put together. Extreme cold, stormy winds, and heavy
> snow, and then, when the thaw set in, the rivers rose so high
> with the floods that three times I was up to my knees in water
> in the carriage. At Holyhead the winds were against me and I
> had to wait for twelve days. Finally, after a ten hours' journey
> by sea, I arrived in port here, where the welcomes and the
> greetings of my friends lessened my sorrow at having had to
> leave Rome.
>
> Sir Nicholas Plunkett immediately invited me to his house
> and put a carriage at my disposal. The Earl of Fingall, who is
> my cousin, invited me to his country seat. The Baron of Louth
> has offered me board and lodging in my own diocese as long
> as I please and I have decided to accept his invitation as he lives
> in the centre of my area. There are also three other knights
> who are married to three cousins of mine and who are vying
> with one another to see which of them can receive me into his
> house.
>
> I was also delighted to find the Bishop of Meath so well and
> so fresh. Though he is sixty-eight years old, he looks no more
> than fifty and has hardly a grey hair on his head. . . .
>
> I made the journey in spite of the bad weather because I
> wanted to be in my province to begin my duties during Lent.
> I shall find it difficult to assemble five priests when
> consecrating the Holy Oils during Holy Week, when all the
> priests are busy hearing confessions: so I would ask your
> Excellency to obtain for me the privilege of consecrating the
> Holy Oils with the assistance of two priests only.

Oliver Plunkett entered his province and his diocese during the
Lent of 1670. He was now Archbishop of the diocese of Armagh,

Metropolitan of the nine dioceses of the Armagh Province, and
Primate of All Ireland. He had the ordinary powers of a bishop
within his own diocese, a more limited power in the other dioceses
of his province, and a very shadowy jurisdiction over the whole
country by virtue of his primacy. His ecclesiastical powers were
extensive but ill-defined and the effort to define them more
accurately was to teach him many a bitter lesson. The clear
distinctions and definitions he had learnt from Canon Law in Rome
had a habit of melting away among the mists of the Irish countryside.

The nobility greeted him with joy, the clergy with sullen
resentment. Neither side knew much about him after his long
absence in Rome except that he was a Plunkett and a Meath man, but
that in itself was enough to open the doors of the one and close the
hearts of the other. In those days the native Irish and the Anglo-Irish
formed two distinct and often opposed camps; the Confederation of
Kilkenny had only papered over the differences and the collapse of
the Confederation not only revealed them again but was in part
caused by them. The Anglo-Irish, who were particularly strong in
County Meath, had what seemed to the native Irish a divided loyalty.
Descended from the Norman conquerors, they were almost all
staunch Catholics and opponents of the Reformation; but at the
same time, they were equally staunch supporters of the English King
and of the English connection.

By his birth and breeding Oliver Plunkett belonged indisputably
to the Anglo-Irish. He mixed on familiar terms with the gentry, he
spoke English as fluently as he did Irish, he accepted without
question that the English King was his lawful sovereign. The great
majority of the clergy in Armagh diocese and in all the province apart
from Meath were of the native Irish with native Irish names and
attitudes; they spoke English with difficulty if they spoke it at all.
They were drawn mainly from the peasantry, most of the Gaelic
landowners having been dispossessed and driven into exile. Their
allegiance to the English King was tenuous and shallow. To them a
Meath man, any Meath man, was someone to be viewed with
suspicion.

It says a great deal for Oliver's tact and judgment that he should
have won over so many of the clergy in so short a time. Barely six

months after his arrival in Armagh, the Vicar-Generals of six of the
northern dioceses wrote a joint letter to Rome thanking the Holy See
for sending so illustrious a Primate to Ireland: 'He is so untiring in
good works and so exemplary in his life and conduct that he has won
for himself and the clergy the love and reverence even of the enemies
of our faith.' They prefaced their remarks by saying that they had
delayed writing until his merits were known to them by experience.

A minority of the clergy, however, both secular and religious,
refused to be won over. During the Cromwellian period the Church
as an organisation had vanished. The priests who had remained
operated on their own, dressed like laity, lived with the laity, were
subject to no superior. To many of them the arrival of a strong and
reform-minded bishop was distinctly unwelcome. Oliver found great
difficulty in trying to restore clerical discipline and he soon singled
out drunkenness as one of the main obstacles to be overcome.

> While visiting six dioceses of this province, I made particular
> efforts to root out the cursed vice of drunkenness, which is the
> parent and nurse of every scandal and dissension. I also
> decreed, under pain of deprivation of benefice, that no priest
> should frequent public houses, drink whiskey, and so on. I
> myself have greatly profited from this decree and, as there is
> little use in preaching without practising, I no longer take a
> drink with my meals. Show me an Irish priest without this vice
> and he is surely a saint.

As Oliver began the systematic visitation of his province, he no
doubt anticipated that he would have to deal with some clerical
abuses. What he had not anticipated was *Praemunire*. 'I must admit,'
he wrote later, 'that when I first came to this kingdom I neither knew
nor understood what was meant by the word *Praemunire*.' He soon
found that is was the Latin name for some old laws that made it an
offence for anyone to exercise any authority derived from the Pope.
This meant, for instance, that if a bishop were to remove a parish
priest or discipline him in any way, he was guilty of *Praemunire* since
his authority as a bishop came from the Pope. He could be taken to

law by the parish priest, found guilty and imprisoned, while the priest continued undisturbed in his previous course of conduct.

Among the most notorious practitioners of this tactic was no less a dignitary than the Vicar-Apostolic of Derry, Terence O'Kelly. Despite his frequently scandalous way of life, all attempts to remove him had failed and he had got more than one of those sent against him imprisoned. Two previous Archbishops had trembled before him, but Oliver did not. He was a Plunkett and he knew that no court would bring in a verdict of guilty on such a trumped-up charge against a personal friend of the Governor of Ulster.

> I went in person to the diocese of Derry, called the clergy together, suspended his jurisdiction, and appointed in his place Dr Conwell, a learned and holy man. I was charged before the civil court, but the unfortunate man found himself forestalled in the Vice-regal court, and in the court of the Governor of Ulster, the Earl of Charlemont. He thereupon cried out in a loud voice: 'The Italian Primate, the Roman Primate, has unhorsed me!'
>
> The Earl of Charlemont has not troubled even one ecclesiastic since I came here. He is so friendly with me that on one occasion, seeing me somewhat afraid, he said to me: 'Have no fear, no one shall dare touch you; and in future do not go to the mountains when you wish to administer confirmations, but come to the courtyard of my palace.' He has made me a present during my lifetime of a garden and excellent orchard, with two fields and a fine house. It is in an excellent position.
>
> As to the Viceroy, everyone know that he has a high opinion of me and has even spoken to the King on my behalf. Dr Brennan, who has my cipher, will tell you more about this. I will only mention here that at my request he reprieved three Catholics who had been tried and sentenced to death in the city of Enniskillen.
>
> The Earl of Drogheda allows me to have a public church with bells, etc., in that part of my diocese that lies inside his territory, which is exempt from royal jurisdiction.

I have been accused before the Viceroy on no fewer than nine occasions in connection with the schools and for having exercised foreign jurisdiction. This nobleman, however, always had these charges brought to his own court and thus they were quashed.

The Viceroy referred to, Lord Berkeley, had been appointed to Dublin in May 1670, two months after Oliver's arrival in Ireland. He got on well with Oliver from the beginning and was a welcome change from his predecessor, the bigoted and intolerant Roberts. During his first two months or so in Ireland, Oliver did not dare appear openly in public but he did not let this unduly restrict his activities. He travelled around under the disguise of an army captain, an unlikely disguise for the scholarly archbishop but perhaps all the more effective for that.

Imagination has to work hard to envisage Oliver in the role of the swashbuckling Captain Brown, a part one would have thought more suited to the talents of an Errol Flynn: clattering into the courtyard of the little country inn, dismounting with a jangle of sword and spurs, quaffing a tankard, singing a song, stealing the customary kiss from the customary buxom serving-wench, then disappearing down the road again in a swirl of dust of hoofbeats. To us these are the tired clichés of the romantic cinema: to Oliver they were, as we shall see, for many weeks a daily reality.

The departure of Roberts meant also the departure of Captain Brown. With the well-disposed Berkeley now ruling Ireland in the King's name, Oliver could go freely about his work. It is a mistake to imagine that he spent all his time in Ireland as a hunted man. There were plenty of anti-Catholic laws on the statute-books but they were not enforced in any systematic way. It was illegal to open a Catholic church or school, but a powerful local magnate like the Earl of Drogheda could ignore the law. It was *Praemunire* for a bishop to exercise his jurisdiction, but a sympathetic magistrate could dismiss the charge or impose a nominal penalty. It all depended on the political climate of the day and much of Oliver's efforts went towards bringing about a suitable climate for the work of the Church and doing as much as possible while it lasted. It is not surprising, in view of his past experiences, that he expressed this in a nautical metaphor.

> This is the time for doing good work, while the present Viceroy is with us. We must follow the example of sailors at sea. When the wind is favourable, they unfurl all their canvas and skim swiftly across the ocean under full sail; but when it turns against them, they lower their sails and take shelter in some little port. While we have the present Viceroy we may sail; and I will do all in my power to advance our spiritual interests, instruct the clergy, and educate them in science and theology.

4

A Man in A Hurry

The first four years of Oliver's primacy, 1670, 1671, 1672 and 1673, were years when the sun shone and the winds blew favourably. Knowing that the weather could change at any moment, Oliver crowded on every possible inch of canvas. He never knew when there might be a change of Viceroys or a change of law or a change of policy and this spurred him to extraordinary activity. Like any man in a hurry, he made occasional mistakes, stepped on occasional toes, made occasional enemies. Still, the record of his achievements during his first six months makes astonishing reading as set out in the letter of the northern Vicar-Generals referred to earlier.

> Since he arrived in the province of Armagh, he has never stopped working. He called together diocesan synods, which were of great benefit to the province, he instructed the clergy by word and example, and in the ordination that he held he ordained only those who were fully worthy and had passed a strict examination.
>
> He held a provincial council in the town of Clones in which many useful decrees were passed; and to the great joy of the clergy and of all Catholics, he suspended the jurisdiction of Terence O'Kelly, Vicar of Derry, a thing which many others had previously attempted without success.
>
> He brought the Fathers of the Society of Jesus into the diocese of Armagh to educate the youth and give instruction to the younger priests, and he built a house and schools for them at his own expense.
>
> In the dioceses of Armagh, Kilmore, Clogher, Derry, Down, Connor and Dromore, in spite of the huge distances involved, he administered confirmation to thousands in the woods and mountains, regardless of winds and rain.

Furthermore, he recently achieved a work that will greatly benefit the whole Catholic community. There were many men of noble family who had lost all their property and been publicly declared outlaws, and who had subsequently been responsible for many crimes of violence. He persuaded them to change their way of life for the better and got them a pardon for their crimes; and not only a pardon for themselves but for all those who sheltered or supported them. In this way hundreds and hundreds of Catholic families have been rescued from great danger to their bodies, souls and properties.

Of the various good works listed, the last-named was the most controversial. A number of dispossessed Catholics had taken to the hills where they led a kind of guerrilla existence and lived by robbing and blackmailing the people of the area around the borders of Armagh and Tyrone. They were known as Tories or Rapparees and at first enjoyed a certain glamour as freedom fighters against the English intruders. But by 1670 the glamour had worn off and the local people had become thoroughly disillusioned with the self-appointed protectors. If they supported the Rapparees, they were harassed, and fined by the government; if they did not, they were liable to be robbed and even murdered by the Rapparees themselves.

Oliver undertook to act as intermediary between the Rapparees and the government. At considerable danger to himself, he met them on the border of County Tyrone and spent an hour talking to them about the dangers to the body and soul that they were bringing upon themselves and their fellow Catholics. He found the unfortunate men at the end of their tether and willing to grasp at any way out of their predicament. Eventually, he succeeded in securing pardons for them and for two of their comrades who were in prison under sentence of death, under condition that they left the country.

The role of the peacemaker is often an ungrateful one. Though the ordinary people of the locality were deeply thankful for the deliverance, he found himself under attack from other sources. The Secretary of Propaganda in Rome, who considered that negotiating with bandits was conduct unbecoming an Archbishop, wrote him a sharp letter of rebuke. Those Rapparees who remained on in various parts of the province denounced him violently as a willing tool of the English in their work of subjugating the Irish. Unkindest cut of all, he was accused at his trial of having been in league with the Rapparees all the time against the English government and of having got them out of the country so that they could organise an army in France for the invasion of Ireland.

The duty of administering the sacrament of confirmation was a less dangerous but much more laborious one. Most of the diocese of Ireland had not had a resident bishop for twenty years and as a result many people, adults as well as children, had never been confirmed. It was Oliver's custom during his visitation of his province to administer the sacrament to the people of each district and to keep careful record of the numbers involved. Since there were few Catholic churches in the country and most of them very small, the confirmation ceremony was usually held in the open air. The Earl of Charlemont, as we have seen, offered the use of his courtyard for this purpose; but in other places, where the local grandee was less helpful or the spies more dangerous, some out-of-the-way wood or mountain valley had to be used.

It is a pity that Oliver has not given us a full description of one of these scenes; probably he had become so accustomed to them that he took the strange surroundings for granted. By the end of 1670 he had covered most of the main centres of population and during 1671 he continued on into the remoter areas, including the mountains of Donegal. When a new Vicar-General was appointed for Raphoe (Donegal), it was Oliver himself who led him through the mountain passes of this not very prepossessing area. In a letter written to Rome soon afterwards, the Vicar-General described his feelings.

> It is for spiritual motives alone that I have taken on the responsibility for so barren, rough and rugged a place. I admit too that I was moved by the words and even more by the example of the illustrious Primate; for he has on many occasions administered confirmation to the children in these very mountains and woods. On many occasions too he has had nothing to eat but oaten bread, salty butter and stirabout, and nothing to drink but milk.

>We are all amazed that a man of such a delicate constitution, who was accustomed (as I myself know) to so many amenities in Rome, should be able to undergo so many labours, so many journeys, so much hardship and adversities. It is quite certain that if he does not change his way of living and acting, he will lose his health and become useless to himself and to others.

It is the first mention we have of Oliver's health; it will not be the last.

Among the many factors that depressed the new Vicar-General of Raphoe, the state of the clergy ranked high. 'The labourers are few,' he wrote, 'and they have little knowledge of the art of arts, that is, the guidance of souls. There are about fourteen priests, of whom only one has ever been outside this country; and he, although he studied in Louvain, is not altogether right in the head. His name is Louis Gallagher. The others had a superficial training in grammar and poetry and some cases of conscience, according to the local custom.'

Oliver himself had become aware of the same problem at an early stage in his journeys, and the question of schools soon became one of his chief concerns. Catholics had now been without schools for twenty years and the lack of education was becoming very apparent among the younger priests and the whole Catholic community. It was obviously impossible for Oliver to provide education on any wide scale but even one well-run school could help to educate an elite, the future clerical and lay leaders of the Catholic community. He set about starting such a school with his customary dispatch, choosing a site in Drogheda where he enjoyed the protection of the Earl and securing the services of two priests of the Society of Jesus, which enjoyed a very high reputation in the field of education. In April 1671 he wrote to Rome to report on progress and ask for financial aid:

>The nobility and gentry of the whole province of Ulster, with only three exceptions, have lost all their lands and from being owners have become tenants; they now have no means to educate their children. The young priests who were ordained during the past seven years to fill the place of those who had died have very little education as they had no one qualified to

teach them; in fact, Catholic teachers were not tolerated at all.

I undertook to deal with the problem. I invited the Jesuit fathers to my diocese; I built a good-sized house for them from the ground up, together with two schools where about 150 boys and 25 clerics are being educated; and for the past nine months I have supported two very learned and hard-working Jesuit, with one lay-brother and one servant.

One of the fathers spends an hour every morning and afternoon giving the clerics instruction in cases of morality and in methods of preaching and teaching catechism; he also teaches the lay pupils for two hours in the morning and another two hours in the evening. On feast days and holidays he teaches the ceremonies and the manner of administering the sacraments, etc. The other Jesuit is occupied in teaching syntax and grammar, etc. In addition, both of them are engaged in preaching. I have supported them for the past nine months and have bought them everything down to the smallest piece of furniture.

Propaganda no doubt had its own problems, and it was not until September of the following year that Oliver received news that money was to be sent for the support of the Jesuits. He wrote at once to express his gratitude and to describe the progress of the school with understandable pride.

I have just received your most welcome letter of the 2nd of September and this whole kingdom is indebted to you for providing the Jesuits with a stipend. They are doing very good work and now have in Drogheda, in my diocese, 160 students. But I had to go through such troubles and make such efforts to support them; and there were so many protests sent to the Viceroy and the Supreme Council against me and against them.

They gave all the more offence to our ill-wishers because they are in Drogheda, which is only four hours' journey from Dublin where no Catholic schools are allowed; and to have

there the Jesuits, whom they hate more than any others, was to
add insult to injury.

Yet now these very same ill-wishers are paying court both to
me and to them in order to get their children into schools; and
in fact they now have many Protestant boys from the leading
families who come to our defence.

Monsignor, I solemnly assure you that I spent more than 400
scudi [£100] on them during the past two years and two
months and we are still in debt for 200 scudi. I dressed in cloth
of a half-scudo a year, I kept only one servant and a boy to look
after my horses, and I cut down on my food, in order to help
the Jesuits. The Viceroy gave me a half promise that he would
not disturb them; but when the money promised by the King
did not arrive, I must admit I found it very difficult to keep
them going and became very depressed in spirits. Now,
however, your letter brings me great joy.

It would appear that some at least of the clerics referred to were
not students but young priests who came to Drogheda to learn after
ordination what they were unable to learn before; in 1673 Oliver
refers to fifty young priests as having benefited from the Jesuit
teachers, who by this time numbered three. He rightly felt that
raising the standard of the clergy was one of the best services he could
give the Irish Church. What Ireland needed was not more priests but
better priests; indeed, from the point of view of mere quantity, the
country had too many. In August of the same year he wrote:

There are too many secular priests here. Every gentleman
wants to have his own chaplain and to have Mass said under
his own roof, under pretext of being afraid of the Government.
They force the bishops to ordain priests and afterwards they
move heaven and earth to obtain a parish for this priest, their
dependent. The remedy for this would be to withdraw from
me and from all the archbishops and bishops of this kingdom
permission to ordain outside the specified times.

The letter goes on to ask for six places in the Irish College for students from three of the northern dioceses. This was a favourite theme of Oliver's. Though conscious of how much the Drogheda schools were doing, he was equally conscious of how much they lacked, especially when compared with the great universities of Rome. He had in an earlier letter already made a request for six places for students in the Propaganda College and given his reasons at length: only a Roman education could fit a priest to occupy a position of leadership in the Church.

Those educated in Rome are better acquainted with the wishes of the Holy See, they know its thinking, they are better able to communicate with it. The Piazza di Spagna, the Propaganda, indeed the whole of Rome, are one great book. There are so many nationalities to be seen there, each with its own customs. Poles, Germans, Spaniards, French, Indians, Turks, Ethiopians, Africans, Americans can be met there; and one learns what skill and judgment are needed to reconcile the various opinions and opposing interests of so many different nationalities.

The changes in the government have also a lesson to teach. One observes the modest and wise and humble behaviour of those who the previous day or under the previous Pope were all-powerful and honoured by everyone: they keep faith equally in prosperity and adversity. I was especially impressed by the prelates Cajetan and Massimi, and another from Modena who had been Governor of Rome in the time of Alexander VII of happy memory, and many others in the time of Innocent and Urban. One comes into contact with cardinals and prelates of great wisdom and prudence, learned and experienced in spiritual affairs and in the temporal affairs of so many rulers and princes. It is impossible for anyone of reasonable ability not to advance greatly in knowledge and experience.

And indeed to educate a missionary priest there is no college in the world better suited than the Propaganda, where the students are instructed for two hours every morning in

theology, and after dinner for an hour in controversy, and later
for half an hour or an hour in cases of conscience. They learn
to preach and to master Hebrew and Greek; they take part in
the Church ceremonies and are trained in Gregorian chant;
they receive in short an education that is better fitted for
missionaries than that of any other college.

Therefore I anxiously implore that I may be allowed to send
half a dozen of the most talented young priests that I can find
to be educated in that college so that my unfortunate province
of Ulster may have men able to govern its churches; for if God
were to take from us in Ulster three men, Thomas Fitzsimons,
Dr Conwell and Dr Ronan Maginn, there would be no one
else with the necessary learning or skill to govern these
churches. The other Vicar-Generals are of no more than
average ability.

If you do not grant me this favour, we shall be without
leaders, without shepherds, and the wolves will devour our
flocks. The Roman – that is, the man educated in Rome – has
the knowledge and the ability to govern. The prince of poets
has fittingly sung:

Tu regere imperio populos, Romane, memento:
Hae tibi erunt artes. . . .

This is one of the most touching and revealing of Oliver's letters
to Rome. There was no need for him to describe the City and its
sights to the Secretaries of a Roman Congregation; he was writing
not for them but for himself. The memories began to flood out as he
wrote and his pen could hardly keep pace with them. The newly
arrived youth in the Piazza di Spagna, gazing at the passing crowds,
seeing perhaps a black man for the first time in his life. The student
in the university corridor arguing in fractured Latin and Italian with
Poles and Germans and Italians and French. The young priest at the
beginning of his career observing how yesterday's dispensers of
patronage became today's forgotten men. The professor in
Propaganda preparing his lectures in theology and controversy for the
eager young missionaries-to-be. The maturing scholar who finds the
perfect quotation from Virgil rising unbidden to his lips: 'Be

mindful, Roman, of thy destiny to rule the peoples with thy sceptre: these shall be thy arts.'

As he sent the letter on its way from his bleak and barbarous nation, a little of his heart went with it.

One would like to now, though, what kind of Americans were to be seen in Rome in the middle of the seventeenth century.

5

UNFINISHED BUSINESS

At the beginning of 1671, with a good deal of his province already visited, Oliver began to make plans for a journey to the islands of Scotland. He had been asked by Propaganda to look after the spiritual needs of the Catholics living in the Hebrides, who spoke a form of Gaelic similar to Ulster Irish, and to appoint some Irish priests to minister there. Oliver found his plans running into difficulties with the Marquis of Antrim, an Irish Catholic nobleman who had succeeded in recovering his estates and was a power in Antrim and the isles. Oliver's letter on the subject showed that he retained both his Roman memories and his sense of humour.

> The visitation of the Hebrides still remains to be done; but if the Sacred Congregation does not write a letter to the Marquis of Antrim, we shall not be able to accomplish anything. This nobleman has great influence in the islands but he has many traits in common with Monsignor Alberici, good and prudent, but slow and cautious about everything. I remember that Monsignor Alberici could not find a servant to suit him in the whole of Italy. From Florence, they were talkative; from Milan, they were giddy; from the Romagna, they were stupid; from Naples, they were light-fingered; from Rome, they were too gloomy.
>
> It is equally difficult to find anyone to please the Marquis of Antrim. I suggested at least twenty priests to him but he had some objection to every one of them; and, about Ronan Maginn, a very suitable man for the task, he remarked that he seemed to be over-hasty and presumptuous and proud. The chief cause of the delay is the treaty of union between Scotland and England, as I mentioned in a previous letter.

The Marquis sent three priests to the islands to administer the sacraments of Penance and the Eucharist during Lent. After Easter they came back, unwilling to stay there all the year round as they had good parishes in County Antrim. Anyhow, they are very old and not able for the hard work of the islands.

A courteous letter to this nobleman, praising his piety and his zeal for the spiritual good of these souls, would be of great help in this affair. I spent three days with him at his home in Dunluce. It is a splendid building. The palace is perched upon a high rock, lashed on every side by the sea. It is only twelve miles distant from the largest of the Hebrides.

Monsignor, this letter is essential, as the Marquis is the only Catholic nobleman who can help me in this mission. Without his assistance I would run many risks.

In June of the same year, he wrote again to ask for money to help with the expenses of his journey to the Hebrides.

I need some assistance to enable me to visit the Scottish islands, that is, the Hebrides. Without your assistance I can do nothing. I shall have to bring a priest and a servant with me and to dress in the kind of clothes worn by the local people, which are different from those worn anywhere else in the world.

The picture of the Archbishop of Armagh dressing himself in kilt and bonnet at the expense of the Vatican is a pleasing one. But it would appear that the projected visit never took place. One reason was the continuing lack of money: in September he informed Propaganda that 'the spirit is willing but the cash is weak.' More important were the political complications referred to in his earlier letter. The visit of an Irish archbishop might be taken as an attempt to stir up the Catholic islanders against the proposed union with England and so bring fresh persecution upon their heads. So Oliver was forced to continue looking after the island people from a distance.

At home there were plenty of other matters to engage his attention. He could not bear the thought of unfinished business. He continued his travels tirelessly and sent a stream of detailed reports to Rome on every place he visited and everyone he met. He sent lists of the names of all the secular priests in the northern dioceses with a short character sketch of each. Most of them were men of blameless lives but occasional exceptions were noted: 'given somewhat to drink', 'weak in doctrine', 'frequents taverns and is under suspicion regarding observance of chastity but has promised reform', 'fathered children as a young man; sent concubine away but is somewhat addicted to drink'.

There were irregularities too among the regular clergy, that is, the religious orders. Of these the Franciscans were by far the most numerous and, by the law of averages, it was only to be expected that most of his troubles with religious involved Franciscans. The friars had shown great heroism during the time of Cromwell and had stuck to their posts through thick and thin; for this they were held in universal respect by the people. But the hard times had taken their toll and discipline had grown lax in some of the smaller communities.

Oliver's attempts at reform were hampered not only by the normal stubbornness of human nature but by the fact that the Franciscans were to a large extent exempt from the authority of the local bishop. He asked without much success for additional powers to deal with them. He complained that they had too many small, badly run novitiates. He complained that Irish Franciscan communities on the continent used Ireland as a dumping place for misfits and malcontents. He complained about the friars questing, that is, asking alms, in parish churches on Sunday; sometimes Mass was held up for hours while friars and farmers haggled over pigs and geese and vegetables. The friars also complained about the meddlesome archbishop and accused him of everything from simony to judicial murder. So tense was the situation that Oliver believed his life to be in danger from one of the friars, Anthony Daly of Armagh. Writing in January 1680 he described a frightening experience of six years earlier.

This Father Anthony made an attempt on my life and instigated the Tories to kill me. They came to the house of my Vicar-General, where I was then staying, around midnight. They burst open the doors and took away all the money from myself and my Vicar-General and my secretary, Michael Plunkett, who is now in Rome, and they held a sword to my throat.

The leader of this band was arrested afterwards. In prison, before his death, he declared to the parish priest in Armagh and to his curate that Father Anthony had told him to kill me and said that he would give him absolution afterwards.

It would be tedious to go into the innumerable ramifications of the innumerable disputes involving the Archbishop and the clergy. It will be sufficient to recount one of the best-known of these, his intervention in the quarrel between the Franciscans and the Dominicans over the ownership of three friaries. He intervened with some reluctance: 'If I decide in favour of the Dominicans, the whole body of the Franciscans will write and publish a thousand accusations and a thousand calumnies against me, saying that this primate is an enemy of the Franciscans, and so on. And vice versa if I decide in favour of the Franciscans.' On instructions from Rome, however, he investigated the affair and after a long and careful inquiry judged in favour of the Dominicans.

His lengthy report on the subject is worth reading in full. It shows his ordered mind at its best, calm, judicial, impartial, cutting away inessentials and marshalling the essential facts in clear and logical order.

I examined the controversy between the Dominicans and Franciscans of the province of Armagh by the authority delegated from Rome as well as by my ordinary authority. I found the arguments put forward by the Dominicans to be the stronger and gave judgment in their favour. The Franciscans however have appealed to the Holy See from my decision and sent a special agent to Rome to present their appeal. Therefore I think it necessary to send Your Excellency an account of the whole matter in as short a space as possible.

The Dominican Fathers of this province have three friaries about which there is no controversy: that is, the friaries of Drogheda, Derry and Bannina or Coleraine. There is no dispute about these. All the controversy is about three other friaries, namely, Newtown in the diocese of Down, Gaula in Clogher, and Carlingford in my own diocese.

I went to the County Down, called together the parties to the dispute, and found the clearest evidence that the friary of Newtown belonged to the Dominicans. St Antoninus makes mention of it in the third part of his history; and Sir James Ware in his book *De Antiquitatibus Hiberniae* says on page 212 about the friary of Down: 'The friary of the Order of Preachers was founded in 1244 and chapters of the order were held there in 1298 and 1312; it is situated in the territory of Ards near the sea-shore.' Moreover, witnesses were produced who swore that they had seen Dominicans of this friary questing in the diocese of Down before the time of Cromwell.

In the diocese of Armagh I summoned before me the parties to the dispute about the friary of Carlingford. The Dominicans again invoked the authority of Ware, who writes on page 203: 'In Carlingford a friary of the Order of Preachers under the patronage of the Earls of Ulster.' They also produced a document of the tenth year of Henry VIII by which a citizen of Carlingford named Mariman made over a house and garden to the Dominicans of the friary of Carlingford. Again, in the Dublin Register called *Defective Titles* there is a mention of this friary of the Dominicans at Carlingford. They also brought forward the evidence of old people who had seen some Dominican friars living near this friary before the war of Cromwell.

I went to the diocese of Clogher and summoned the contending parties to the Franciscan Friary near Enniskillen. The Dominicans adduced the authority of the ancient annals of that town, written in the Irish language, which give the name of the friary of Gaula, the year in which it was founded, and the name of the Pope under whom it was founded for the Dominicans. They brought forward in addition an old priest who swore that he heard from his father that the friary of Gaula belonged to the Dominicans. They also produced other witnesses who gave similar evidence.

The Franciscans, on the other hand, could bring forward nothing but negative evidence. They produced the signatures of people who testified that they had never seen or heard of the Dominicans being in these friaries. They claimed that the people were not able to support both Dominicans and Franciscans. They said that the secular clergy were opposed to the Dominicans. They went around collecting the signatures of the gentry and others against the Dominicans and they went so far as to approach Protestant gentlemen and ask them to speak to me against the Dominicans. Many of these did in fact speak to me and virtually threatened me if I did not remove the Dominicans from these dioceses.

The Franciscans argued finally that the Dominicans, even if they once owned these friaries, had lost all right to them as they had abandoned and deserted them for many years, so that prescription now held against them. The Dominicans, however, replied that in time of war, pestilence and persecution, no prescription holds good against those who abandon their friaries.

These were in essence the principal arguments on either side that, with the whole of the proceedings, I submitted to the Bishop of Meath, to Dr Thomas Fitzsimons, Vicar-General of Kilmore, and to Dr Oliver Dease, Vicar-General of Meath. They were of the opinion that I should decide in favour of the Dominicans and I did so.

Here it must be remarked that the Dominicans came to live in these dioceses near these friaries upon the restoration of the King and the ending of Cromwell's persecution, that is, seven or eight years before I came to this country; so I did not introduce them here but found them already in possession.

Considering, then, the arguments brought forward by the Dominicans and considering that I found them already in possession of their residences in these dioceses; considering too the great good that they do, having able preachers and learned men among them; finally, considering that both orders have sufficient for their support in these dioceses since they supported themselves here for the last ten years in spite of their disputes, and could support themselves far better if they lived at peace, since many people are so scandalised at their quarrels that they will give alms to neither; in consideration of all these things I deemed myself bound in conscience to give judgment in favour of the Dominicans.

On publication of the verdict, the Franciscans appealed to the Holy See and it seemed as if all Hell broke loose upon me. Among the accusations, it was said that I gave judgment without listening to both sides; yet the Very Reverend Paul O'Neill, who goes as their representative to Rome, was present when I heard both sides in the diocese of Dromore, as were also Dr Ronan Maginn, Vicar-Apostolic of Dromore, and twenty other priests and friars. In the diocese of Clogher, the inquiry was held in the friary of the Franciscans themselves; and while I was holding this session I got a severe attack of illness.

As to my own diocese, everyone knows that I heard them. The crowd that assembled was so large, even though some miles distant from the city, that it requires downright barefacedness to say that I did not examine the matter. Still, they threaten me time and again that they will treat me as they treated my predecessor, Richard of Armagh, who was summoned to Avignon and died there of grief. The guardian of Dundalk told me this to my face.

It is unnecessary for me to say any more as Your Excellency is both wise enough and concerned enough to settle the matter properly. I would ask you to show this letter, as also all my other letters, to Dr Peter Creagh, our agent in Rome, to keep him informed of the affairs of the province, and I shall ever remain,

Your most obliged and obedient servant,
Oliver of Armagh
Dundalk, 8 September 1672

The violent reaction of the Franciscans in Ireland was re-echoed abroad. In the library of Saint Isidore's, the Irish Franciscan House in Rome, a bust of the Archbishop had recently been set up. Two of the students, John McMoyer and Hugh Duffy, demonstrated their feelings on the subject by knocking the head off the bust. For this they were expelled but afterwards gained admission to the Franciscan novitiate in Spain and eventually returned to Ireland. Nine years later they were to have their revenge.

One other point worth mentioning in the letter is the reference to Oliver's illness. We are given no clue as to its nature and he refers to it not for its own sake but to refute the suggestion that he had not held a proper inquiry; obviously his illness during the inquiry had been a talking-point and had fixed the event in everyone's mind. There can be little doubt, however, that the Archbishop's health was beginning to deteriorate under the constant strain to which he was subjected.

6

THE TWO PRIMATES

There was one ecclesiastical controversy that had a rather special character in that it involved Oliver not with the lower clergy but with an equal, or at least one who claimed to be an equal. This was Peter Talbot, Archbishop of Dublin, who had initially welcomed the appointment of the new Archbishop of Armagh but had since come to revise his opinion.

The work of re-establishing the hierarchy begun in 1669 had been taken a step further in 1671 with the appointment of another six bishops. Among them was Oliver's old friend, John Brennan, whom he had left behind in Rome and who now returned to Ireland as Bishop of Waterford. The country now had a hierarchy of four archbishops and eight bishops; and at the head of that hierarchy, by immemorial custom, was the Archbishop of Armagh in his capacity of Primate of All Ireland.

That was Oliver Plunkett's view of the situation, a view not shared by Peter Talbot.

Talbot was a colourful cleric, even in that age of colourful clerics. He came from an Anglo-Irish family every bit as distinguished as Oliver's but his career had followed very different lines. An ardent royalist, he had joined the Jesuits, and, during the period when Cromwell ruled England, had attached himself to the exiled Charles II. All governments in exile live by plot and counter-plot; intrigue is their life-blood, rumour is the air they breathe. Talbot loved every minute of it and was constantly engaged in cloak-and-dagger missions for his royal master, all of them unfathomably mysterious but of the highest importance. One would be tempted to describe him as the typical Jesuit of fiction but for the fact that he found his membership of the Society hampering his work and resigned to join the secular clergy. Charles did not forget his faithful henchman when restored to the English throne and it was partly at his urging that Talbot was appointed to the See of Dublin in 1669.

The first clash between the two archbishops occurred at the Synod held in Dublin in June 1670. Reviving a half-forgotten historical claim, Talbot sought to preside at the Synod on the grounds that the Archbishop of Dublin was Primate of Ireland. Oliver contested this claim on the grounds that his bull of appointment gave him the title of Primate while Talbot's did not. Talbot further complicated the issue by claiming to have a document from the King appointing him head of the Irish hierarchy in civil affairs, but was either unable or unwilling to produce it. It was finally agreed to let Oliver preside and refer the matter to Rome for a decision.

These matters should have rested but did not. Throughout 1671 the dispute about the primacy simmered on. The followers of the two archbishops continued to argue the case, with the inevitable result of driving the principals further apart. Both wrote to Rome complaining about the activities of the other. Oliver was worried that Talbot's continuing political intrigues were threatening the peace of the Church in Ireland; he had already antagonised the tolerant Viceroy, Berkeley, and was in danger of being exiled. In March 1671 Oliver wrote:

> The Viceroy, who in any event has little love for Dr Talbot and his family, had for these and other reasons made up his mind to banish him from the kingdom. I did everything in my power to dissuade the Viceroy and humbly begged him not to take this course of action. At the same time, I assured him that whatever difference there might be between the Archbishop of Dublin and myself over the question of jurisdiction, we were still friends. His Excellency was appeased and said he was edified by my intervention of behalf of Dr Talbot.

Talbot and his supporters were by no means behind-hand in making counter-accusations against the Archbishop of Armagh. They told Rome that he was imprudent and autocratic, that he had acted rashly in setting up schools and becoming involved with the Tories, that he was over-friendly with the Protestants and particularly with the Duke of Ormond (an old enemy of the Talbot family). All this was routine stuff; but Roman eyebrows must have been raised when the further accusation was made that Dr Plunkett's relations with women were causing scandal and that he had been guilty of sexual misconduct on a number of occasions.

This was too much. Oliver wrote indignantly to answer the charges; but his answer must have caused even more astonishment in Rome that the original accusations:

> I said some time ago that if I published the decree in favour of the Dominicans there would be no end to the slanders made against me. I assure Your Excellency that since the present Viceroy came to this kingdom (that is, during the past two years), no living being can accuse me of having done anything unbecoming my sacred office. I ask you to note this statement carefully. Yes; distinguish the times and you shall reconcile the scriptures.
>
> During the time of the previous Viceroy, Roberts, who pursued me with great hostility, I was forced to conceal myself by going around under the name of Captain Brown, with a sword and wig and pistols and so on; this lasted for two or three months. When I visited a house or went into a tavern, I used to kiss the women, I used to sing, and on one occasion when some non-Catholics with me seemed suspicious of my identity, I took up on my horse with me the wife of the gentleman in whose house I was then staying and we rode together for a mile accompanied by the lady's brother, who was a Catholic. All this took place two years ago. I ask you therefore to read these accusations carefully and to be on your guard if the writer speaks in general terms.

One would dearly love to know how this letter was received in the Sacred Congregation for the Propagation of the Faith. Discreet archiepiscopal amours they had encountered before, but this kind of behaviour was totally outside their experience. It seemed to have all the disadvantages of a public scandal without any of the private compensations. What exchanging was there of remarks and glances, what helpless shrugging of soft monsignorial shoulders, what raising of brown Italian eyes to Heaven? Or had they by now reached the stage where nothing they read in any letter from Ireland could surprise them any more?

Almost simultaneously with the arrival of this letter in Rome in the late spring of 1672 came others from Ireland reporting on the latest exploit of the unpredictable Primate. A book had just appeared in Dublin, entitled *Jus Primatiale* or *The Ancient Right and Preheminency of the See of Armagh above all Archbishopricks in the Kingdom of Ireland.* The author's name was veiled under the initials O.A.T.H.P. but it required no great power of divination to interpret this as *Oliverius Armacanus Totius Hiberniae Primas,* that is, Oliver of Armagh, Primate of All Ireland.

This short work has a special interest as the only formal piece of literature written by Oliver. It is a slim, small volume, the pages measuring just over six inches by four. It is written in English, but with plentiful quotations from Latin documents, and it opens with a five-page introduction in which the writer declares his aim of rescuing Armagh's primacy 'from the Worm of Oblivion, which often proveth to be the Mother of Ignorance'.

There are seventy-five pages in the main body of the book and a seventy-sixth is devoted to correcting errata. The opening pages may be quoted in full as they show once again Oliver's knack of getting straight to the essence of his subject and of answering the reader's questions before he has time to ask them. The spelling and punctuation have been brought into line with modern usage; otherwise it is as Oliver wrote it.

> The first occasion of the difference between the Archbishop of Armagh and the Archbishop of Dublin concerning precedency and other points of superiority and jurisdiction happened in a meeting of all the archbishops and bishops of the Roman Catholic profession in the month of June 1670, in Dublin, when they were subscribing a remonstrance of their loyalty to be presented to his Excellency the Lord Berkeley, each of them refusing to subscribe subsequently to the other; which contestation did displease many, both in this Kingdom and in foreign countries, for the three ensuing reasons.

First, they are and were in a country governed and for the most part inhabited by those of a contrary profession.

Secondly, prelates of the Church in giving honour ought to go one before the other, not in seeking honour.*

Thirdly, that archbishops and bishops should increase their reputation by modesty and not by ambition.

I confess these to be good and sound reasons and ought to move the ecclesiastical superiors to all modesty and humility, consistent with the honour and jurisdiction of the prelacy they exercise; but to prejudice the dignity of the See committed to their charge and also their successors would render them odious to all posterity, and argue breach of trust and weakness in them; and therefore, from the very time of the Apostles to this day, both ecclesiastical and secular superiors strived to maintain the right of the dignities and offices imposed on them.

The author then cites a number of instances of eminent clerics engaging in disputes about precedence, before passing on to the main argument. An impressive array of authorities is quoted, including the ancient life of St Patrick by Jocelinus and a bull of Pope Urban IV in 1263. Talbot himself is referred to only indirectly, and then more in sorrow than in anger: 'It is a doleful thing that passion should alter the judgments of great men, as Aristotle saith in his Rhetorics.' The work ends with the pious hope that attempts to challenge the primacy of Armagh 'shall have no effect for the future to prejudice the pre-eminency of that ancient and most illustrious See in its superiority over all other archbishoprics in this Kingdom of Ireland.'

There is no doubt that Oliver believed he was in the right not only in defending the primacy of Armagh but in defending it at that time and in that way. He was conscious of the arguments in favour of silence and had consciously rejected them. The primacy of his See had been maintained for more than a thousand years and it was his clear and bounden duty to continue to maintain it. He would not

---

* The meaning of this is that prelates of the Church ought to outdo one another in giving honour, not in seeking it.

shirk that duty, no matter what pain or scandal he might cause others by doing so.

The pained and the scandalised naturally included the Archbishop of Dublin, who wrote at once to complain of Oliver's 'imprudence and inconsistency'. More significantly, they included one reasonably impartial observer, Dr John Brennan, the newly arrived Bishop of Waterford. Despite his old friendship with Oliver, he did not conceal his dismay at the course events were taking. He sent Rome an account of what he called a 'noisy and scandalous dispute'.

> While I was in Dublin I tried discreetly but persistently to reconcile them, and I tried to do the same by writing from here. All I succeeded in getting was fair promises and a superficial patching-up of differences. I will keep on doing everything in my power but without much hope since both of them are hot-tempered and the dispute has now become public in England as well as in Ireland. As a result, most of the Catholics are divided in favour of one or other. I have also been told by an important person that in Dublin the Protestant ministers are talking with great delight about this controversy, even from the pulpits.

In a letter to the Internuncio in Brussels a few days later, Brennan used similar terms about the two disputants: 'they are both of them touchy and hot-tempered'. Of all the countless accusations made against Oliver to the Roman Curia, this is the only one that strikes home. It was made not by an enemy but by a friend of twenty-five years' standing and it was made not once but twice in the measured language of official reports. If John Brennan described him as touchy and hot-tempered then we can safely take it that he was touchy and hot-tempered.

In November of that year Oliver wrote to the Internuncio to report that he and Talbot had settled their differences.

> Through the efforts of the Bishop of Killaloe, perfect harmony has been restored between the Archbishop of Dublin and

myself. Dr Talbot, his brothers and nephews, and I, all had dinner together; and in the evening Dr Talbot and his brothers came to visit all my friends, something that has not happened this past twelve months. We shall send all documents relating to the controversy to Rome and shall await a decision in peace and tranquillity.

John Brennan was less optimistic. 'The Archbishops of Armagh and Dublin have been getting along smoothly since their reconciliation,' he wrote in January 1673, 'but I doubt if it will last very long.' His prophecy was never tested. Before the end of the year, Talbot was to be in exile, Plunkett and Brennan in hiding, and the dispute about the primacy thrust back into the obscurity from which it should never have emerged.

7

FLIGHT IN WINTER

In August 1672, the friendly Viceroy Berkeley (whose wife, Oliver discovered, was a Catholic) had been replaced by the Earl of Essex. Essex was a complex man, conscientious but irresolute; he was prepared to continue Berkeley's policy of toleration as long as he was free from outside pressures. But Ireland could never be long unaffected by events in the neighbouring island and the year 1673 was marked by an outburst of anti-Catholic feeling in England that pitted an increasingly Protestant Parliament against an increasingly Catholic court. The revelation that the Duke of York, the King's brother and heir to the throne, had been for years a secret Catholic caused a storm in Parliament. The Duke was forced to resign from his post of Lord High Admiral and the King promised a stricter enforcement of the laws against Popery.

Essex had no choice but to follow the lead of his royal master. On October 27 an edict was issued that closed all Catholic schools and religious houses and banished all Ordinaries (that is, bishops and vicar-generals) and all regular clergy from the country. They were ordered to register at one of the designated sea-ports and wait there until a vessel was ready to take them to exile on the Continent.

The simple thing to do was to register and then hope that the normal inertia of Irish administration would prevent any further action being taken. The ageing Patrick Plunkett, Bishop of Meath, gave in his name at Dublin, as did the Bishop of Killaloe; the Archbishop of Tuam registered in Galway, and others elsewhere.

Oliver decided not to register. It was his first clear and open flouting of the law. Up to this he had been operating in the shadowy area between legality and illegality, relying on personal contacts here, family influence there, to smooth things over. Now he realised that the old-boy network that had protected him so far was beginning to unravel and cold winds from across the Channel were breaking up

the cosy family world of Irish politics. He had tried cooperation as
long as cooperation had helped his work; now he would try defiance.

It was an unexpected decision, a courageous decision, and it
involved a new development in Oliver's character. He was now one
of the best known people in Irish life and he had no hope of being
able to go around in disguise; he would have to go underground.
Methodically, he collected his books and candles and made his plans,
and on 12 November 1673, he reported those plans to Propaganda.

> The government here is terrified of the anti-Catholic
> Parliament and dare not offer any leniency in our sentence of
> banishment or postpone putting it into effect beyond 1
> December. I have urged my colleagues to stand firm and not
> to abandon their flocks but to follow the example of the
> bishops of the first three centuries and retire to some corner of
> their districts until the storm blows over.
>
> I shall retire to some little hut in the woods or mountains of
> my diocese with a supply of candles and books. You can go on
> sending me letters as usual, however, and I will try to send you
> some information from time to time. Please be so kind as not
> to send envelopes as they cost me so much as the letters
> themselves; every letter with an envelope costs 46 bajocchi,
> without the envelope it would only cost 23 bajocchi.

In a postscript he added: 'The Bishop of Waterford will come to
my district to go into hiding, as his own city is full of fanatics and
furious Presbyterians.' The decision of John Brennan to travel the
length of the country in order to join Oliver in Armagh is surprising
and the explanation given is hardly the whole story. It looks as
though Brennan, a man somewhat lacking in self-confidence, sought
comfort in Oliver's companionship and strength in his leadership at
this difficult time.

By mid-December the two bishops had gone to their hiding-place
and from there Oliver succeeded in sending a further report to Rome.
The worst news was the closing down, apparently for ever, of his
dearest project, the school in Drogheda; in comparison with that, his
own tribulations counted for little.

Things are very bad here and, with another meeting of Parliament due on 7 January next, they may get worse. I am in hiding and Dr Brennan is with me. The Catholic laity are in such great fear of having their property confiscated that no one who has anything to lose will give shelter to any Ordinary or religious; and although the latter are being to some extent connived at, yet the Catholics hardly even dare let them into their houses to say Mass. The bishops or ordinaries can get nothing from the priests. I sometimes find it difficult even to get oaten bread; and the house where Dr Brennan and I are staying is made of straw and covered or thatched so badly that we can see the stars when we are in bed and even the lightest shower of rain sprinkles our pillows. But we are resolved to die from hunger and cold rather than abandon our flocks. It would be a shame for spiritual soldiers, educated in Rome, to become hirelings. We shall take no step without the order of Your Eminences.

The thing that has caused me the greatest sorrow is to see the destruction of the schools I founded, after so much hard work had gone into them. We have so many talented young Catholics: what are they to do now?

Worse was yet to come, as a letter dated 27 January 1674 reported to the Internuncio in Brussels. Mgr Falconieri had no difficulty in recognising the handwriting, though for reasons of security Oliver no longer dared give either his own name or that of his companion.

About the 10th of this month the Viceroy published a further proclamation ordering that the full rigour of the law was yet to be applied to the clergy who had registered. Another order, this one secret, was given to all the magistrates and sheriffs to put their spies on the track of the remaining bishops and regulars, both in the cities and in the countryside.

As soon as my companion and I heard of this we thought it necessary to take to our heels. It was after vespers on Sunday, the 18th of this month (old style), the Feast of Saint Peter's Chair. The snow was falling very heavily, mixed with hailstones which were very hard and large. There was a cutting north wind blowing into our faces and it beat the snow and hail so fiercely into our eyes that even now we are hardly able to see with them. Many times we were in danger of being lost in the valleys and of dying of suffocation in the snow.

Finally we arrived at the house of a gentleman who had lost so much he had nothing more to lose. As ill-luck would have it, however, he had a stranger staying in the house whom we did not want to recognise us, so we were placed in a large attic without either chimney or fire where we have been for the last eight days: may it all work for the glory of God and the salvation of our souls and the flocks entrusted to our charge.

The cold and the hail were so terrible that my eyes have not yet stopped running nor have those of my companion. I feel that I shall lose more than one tooth, they are paining me so much, and my companion was attacked with rheumatism in one arm and can scarcely move it.

In brief, we may truly say that our flight was in winter and on a sabbath*, that is, on Sunday, and on the Feast of Saint Peter's Chair. Blessed be God who granted us the favour of suffering not only for the Chair of Peter but on the very day dedicated to the feast of that chair that rests on a rock and will in the end, I hope, break the violence of these tempestuous waves.

So far I have not heard of anyone being arrested, apart from a certain Father Eugene Cogley of the Order of Saint Dominic, Prior of Tuam, and a Father Francis Brennan in Mullingar; but I am afraid that before long there will be so many arrests that there will be no room left in the prisons, since I have been told that the sheriffs and magistrates of the King have been ordered to hunt out the bishops and regulars and even to search private houses. God help us all.

I make you my reverence.

Thomas Cox

27 January (old style) 1674

---

*   The reference is to Mt 24:20, 'Pray that your flight may not be in winter or on a sabbath.'

That experience on the mountain-side, in darkness and in snow, was clearly a terrifying one. During the days that followed in the cheerless, fireless attic, Oliver had plenty of time to reflect on his close escape from death. Then came news that Catholics in Scotland were to be liable to the penalty of high treason. Had he escaped death from cold and exposure in order to die a still more painful one by the knife of the executioner? The good shepherd laid down his life for his flock while the hireling ran away: was this the choice he was being asked to make? He brushed the thought aside: under the law of the Kingdom of Ireland he was liable to imprisonment or exile but nothing worse. He had never been guilty of treason and never would be.

Here we are in greater fear and trembling than ever, for our neighbour's house is on fire. In Scotland the Parliament enacted that in future it should be considered high treason to hear Mass. It would seem that the days of Nero and Domitian and Diocletian have returned; the penalty for this crime of high treason is to be disembowelled and quartered. So we shall have the blood of martyrs in abundance to fertilise the Church. . . .

It is like the time of the early Church; and it is my hope that the Church will once again be made glorious and enriched by the sufferings and martyrdoms of her northern children who are humble and devoted servants and imitators of Christ and the Apostles, and that the adverse storm will help us even more than the favouring breeze.

These edicts and proclamations and decrees do not as yet apply to Ireland since it is not expressly mentioned in them; but as usual I do not think there is much danger that they will overlook us. If they come to us, then God be praised, we shall welcome them, whether we have to suffer or die. At all events, we shall not be hirelings. We shall not abandon the sheep or the lambs until they drag us to the boat with ropes around our necks.

I beg you to obtain for us the prayers of the servants of God, that he may protect us from the assembly of the wicked and grant us the gift of holy perseverance.

I am with all reverence you most obliged and devoted servant.

Thomas Cox

12 February 1674

In the event, this particular storm abated, though neither quickly nor completely. None of the bishops was exiled that winter except Peter Talbot of Dublin, and he more for his political than for his religious activities. Having impressed the English Parliament with a great noise of anti-Catholic edicts, nearly everyone, from the Viceroy down, was content to let the matter go no further. The clergy who had registered waited in the ports while the ships were delayed by increasingly mysterious obstacles. Eventually they quietly went back to their dioceses and their religious houses. One group of friars in New Ross was actually put on board a ship and dispatched in the direction of France; but ten miles down the estuary, out of sight of the town, the friars were put on land again and rapidly disappeared from view. It was enough to make Cromwell turn in his grave.

In one sense, then, Oliver gained nothing by his miserable winter except an eye complaint that lasted the rest of his life. He could have spent the same time in comfort at Sir Nicholas Plunkett's home in Dublin, a law-abiding citizen, waiting ostentatiously for the ship that never came. But in another sense, the gains were quite incalculable. He had made the distinction between what was expedient and what was right in the clearest and most public possible terms. He had laid down the principle for himself, and through his example for others, that no Irish bishop could consent to accept exile unless bodily carried on board ship. The émigré hierarchy of the 1660s was a thing of the past: from now on Irish bishops would stay with their flocks and, if necessary, die with them.

8

WRITING IN FOUR LANGUAGES

Things gradually returned to something like normal, though it was not until 1675 that Oliver felt free to move around openly again. All the time the cold eye of the English Parliament was upon the Irish Papists and things that were possible a couple of years before had now become impossible again. The Drogheda schools never re-opened and Catholic education soon returned to its former unsatisfactory state. Oliver's activities seem to have become restricted in other areas too; certainly the number of his letters in the Roman archives for the years 1675 to 1679 is much less than that for the preceding period.

This may be a convenient point at which to say something about Oliver's writings. Oliver spoke four languages, English, Irish, Latin and Italian, and wrote in at least three of them (his Irish writings are of doubtful authenticity). The language in which he wrote most easily was not English but Italian, in which his twenty-three years' residence in Rome had given him great fluency. The great bulk of his letters to Rome and Brussels were written in Italian, though there were occasional letters, mostly of a more formal kind, in Latin. No one in the Roman Curia apparently had any knowledge of English, much less Irish.

It is amazing how Oliver found time, among all his other activities, to write so many and such long letters. He wrote regularly to the other Irish bishops so as to be able to keep Propaganda informed of the whole Irish situation. He frequently sent more than one copy of an important letter, in case it was lost or intercepted on the way. He suspected Dublin Castle of tampering with his mail and his suspicions were dramatically confirmed in 1671 during an interview with Lord Berkeley. The Viceroy told him, among other things:

> That many letters of Airoldi and Baldeschi had been intercepted but that they gave great satisfaction to the

government. Then he said, with emphasis: 'If you follow their good advice and avoid meddling in political or civil matters, you have no more annoyance from the King.' He also said that he had seen the printed instructions that are given to missionaries and approved of them, especially the last one, which urged them not to write about any temporal or political matters.

He also said that some of my letters to Airoldi and Baldeschi had been intercepted and that he always found them making highly complimentary reference to himself, for which he thanked me. I said that they contained no more than the truth. He went on to say that he had had all these letters carefully sealed and put back in the post, and that he had given orders that no more letters of mine were to be intercepted or brought to him. I gave him infinite thanks for this, and took my leave after many expressions of politeness.

Despite the Viceroy's assurances, this extraordinary interview must have made Oliver more cautious than ever about what he wrote in his letters.

Airoldi was the Internuncio in Brussels, who had a kind of watching brief over English and Irish affairs; Baldeschi was the Secretary of the Congregation for the Propagation of the Faith, know for short as Propaganda. Oliver sent all his letters to Brussels, addressed to Airoldi under the pseudonym of M. de Pruisson, and Airoldi sent them on to Rome; similarly, Baldeschi transmitted his letters to Oliver through Airoldi. Airoldi seems to have been an amiable and tactful intermediary between the touchy Archbishop and the imperious Secretary, who did not always see eye to eye. At first, Baldeschi thought Oliver headstrong and meddlesome; snowed under by the sudden avalanche of indignant letters from Oliver's opponents, he surfaced to fire off an occasional barbed arrow in the direction of Armagh. The following may serve as an example of Baldeschi's epistolary style, its particular tone of silken insolence obviously the result of many years of practice. It is dated 27 September 1670.

> It must be the Irish climate that has caused Your Excellency to forget the customary forms and regulations of this Curia. I am astonished you should not remember that it is impossible for you to obtain the faculty of dismissing from their order Franciscans who have made their profession.
>
> These lapses of memory, my dear Monsignor, are considered over here to be due to the fact that you are forgetting to apply yourself to spiritual matters as you ought and have instead become totally immersed in temporal affairs.

It would appear that Airoldi thought it prudent to forget to send on some of Baldeschi's letters and that this was one of them. In any event, Baldeschi soon came to a juster estimate of the Archbishop and, in the matter of the Tories, went so far as to admit that he was wrong and Oliver right.

On the whole, Oliver reacted fairly mildly to these and similar rebukes. Apart from his natural respect for Roman institutions, he was no doubt influenced by the fact that Baldeschi held the not inconsiderable Roman purse-strings. The Drogheda schools had been largely supported by Propaganda and there were many other expenses for which Oliver sought help from Rome. Among these was the expense of the letters themselves. A letter of 15 September 1674 to the new Internuncio Falconieri speaks with some feeling about the matter.

> If I had served the Duke of Mirandola in letter-writing and otherwise as I served the Sacred Congregation in the last five years, my baker's bill would long ago have been settled. If I had the means I would spare no pains in serving their Eminences, being bound to do so by every law of justice and gratitude; but what I cannot do, I cannot do.
>
> Every single letter that I send to Your Excellency costs me one giulio, each letter I receive from you costs me 2$^{1}/_{2}$ giuli. Any time I get a letter from Cashel or Tuam it costs me a carlino in Dublin and then 2$^{1}/_{2}$ bajocchi from Dublin to where I live.

Then I have to pay my agents in Dublin and London, who have to go to the post to get the letters and send them on to me, and I could not be niggardly in paying them. They would not have done me this service, using their time and their shoes and their paper and their ink, if I had not been generous with them. The same is true of my correspondents in Tuam and Cashel, and indeed they were worthy of their hire.

I am sure that Your Excellency's purse also feels the expense of letters. Every year it has cost me at least 100 scudi and since you came to the Nunciature in Flanders it has cost me more than 100 scudi; because all during the persecution, which has now lasted eleven months, I was hidden in the mountains with the Bishop of Waterford, at least until two months ago; yet I always managed to keep up my correspondence, in spite of the difficulties.

The carlino, giulio and bajocco were small coins, but 100 scudi was equivalent to £25, a very large sum in those days. It must be remembered that there were no government postal services then such as we have now. Letters were handled by a network of agents, each one expecting his commission, and letters for abroad had to wait until a ship was ready to sail. Whenever Oliver was in or near a seaport he took the opportunity to send off some foreign mail. Usually this was Dublin, but on one occasion he wrote from Galway and had to apologise for the sorry state of the letter. 'I beg you to excuse the smears on this letter, as the servant knocked over the bottle of ink when making my bed. The post leaves in two hours and is some distance away, so I have no time to re-write the letter.'

His style, like his handwriting, reads strong and serviceable and clear. As none of his letters were intended as literary exercises, there are no purple patches and no striving after effect. When he had time to compose his thoughts, he could marshal facts and arguments in a very masterly fashion. But usually his letters were dashed off in a hurry to catch the post and they contain the mistakes and disproportions and lack of order of any hastily written document. Oliver was well aware of these defects and one of his letters to the Internuncio ends with the altogether charming apology, 'I beg you to excuse the prolixity of this letter, for I had not enough time to make it shorter.' At first reading one imagines that he has made a mistake, then one realises he means exactly what he says.

Little need be said about his writings in Latin, which are mainly short formal documents; his Latin is correct but awkward, with little feeling for the language. But he shows familiarity with the works of the masters of Latin literature and quotes from Virgil, Horace, Ovid and Boethius. All his scripture quotations and references are given in the Latin of the Vulgate version, whether the rest of the letter is in Italian or in English; and since scriptural allusions abound in his writings, one comes across a Latin phrase or sentence every few lines.

His writing in English is noticeably less fluent than in Italian. This is surprising, since he presumably spoke English from his earliest years; in all likelihood he spoke English to his family and social equals, Irish to servants and tenants. During his long years in Rome, however, he probably wrote little in either language and lost some of his facility. In the introduction to his book on the primacy, he makes the request to the reader 'that you expect not in this treatise the style of an orator well versed in the English tongue, wherein I acknowledge my weakness, but regard the substance of the subject matter in question'. The style of the book is better than this would lead one to expect, rugged but clear, but his sentences tend to become long and involved in a manner more suggestive of Latin than of modern English.

Anyhow, for Oliver style was an irrelevancy. The important thing was what was said, not how it was said. In a postscript to one of the last letters he ever wrote, he apologised to Father Corker for his rough style: but the apology has a ring of pride about it.

> My language and words are rude. I never hunted after flourishes in any language. Words are signs, *sunt enim signa seu notae eorum conceptuum seu passionum quae sunt in animo**, as the philosopher saith. Many taverns have fair and majestical signs though there be no good liquor in the cellar. But I know

---

*   They are signs or marks of those concepts and passions that are in the mind.

you are like those travellers who had rather enter to an inn furnished with good wine, though it had but a withered ill-shaped sign, than to lodge at a tavern full of corrupted and adulterated liquors, although adorned with a lofty, gilded, and fairly painted sign, whose sight allures all passengers to light but they never return again; and even as gallant signs doth not feed the passenger's belly, so words do not feed the hearer's or reader's brain or understanding, who is by solid enthymemes and syllogisms comforted and nourished.

Finally, some mention must be made of Oliver's writing in Irish. Nothing survives in his own handwriting, but there are two quatrains that have been attributed to him. One is a rather bitter epigram on the priests of the time:

Sagairt óir is cailís chrainn
  Bhí le linn Phádraig i n-Éirinn;
Sagairt chrainn is cailís óir
  I ndeire an domhain dearóil.

Priests of gold and chalices of wood
  Were Ireland's lot in Patrick's time of old;
But now the latter days of our sad world
  Have priests of wood and chalices of gold.

If not actually written by him, these lines may well have been quoted by him. Events certainly gave him cause for a somewhat jaundiced view of the contemporary priesthood.

The other four-line stanza is addressed to Tara, where the palace of the High King of ancient Ireland once stood. It was written on seeing a person cutting grass on that venerable site, and may form part of a longer poem.

A Theamhair na rí, dob annamh leat,
  Re linn Chormaic mhic Airt mhic Cuinn,
Alt riabhach do bhodach bhocht
  Bheith ag gearra guirt ar do dhruim.

Tara of Kings, how strange for thee,
  In Cormac Mac Art's far distant day,
To feel upon thy back the fist
  Of some rough peasant cutting hay.

These lines, if they are genuine, show that Oliver had more feeling for the history and traditions of Gaelic Ireland than his birth and upbringing would suggest.

9

THE STORM GATHERS

The uneasy peace continued in Ireland, though London seethed with rumour and intrigue. Tension grew between the King and the Parliament, and the King's opponents found an able and unscrupulous leader in the Earl of Shaftesbury. Shaftesbury was not particularly anti-Catholic but he was happy to use any weapon, however dishonourable, to break the power of the monarchy. The King's wife and brother were Catholics and the King was only waiting a favourable opportunity of becoming a Catholic himself; so it was clear enough to Shaftesbury that by playing on the anti-Catholic suspicions of the mob he could easily arouse them against the royal family. A variety of fantastic rumours were put into circulation, anti-Popery demonstrations were organised, and the Catholics were accused of having caused everything from the execution of Charles I to the Great Fire of London.

Some time early in the year 1676 a down-at-heel clergyman by the name of Titus Oates arrived in London. Though still in his twenties, he had already had various brushes with the law for crimes ranging from perjury to sodomy. He was as repulsive in body as he was in mind, squat, bull-necked, bow-legged, with a voice like the braying of a donkey. His complexion was vermillion in colour, his eyes sunken and pig-like, and his chin so large that it almost equalled all the rest of his face put together. 'His mouth was the centre of his face,' wrote one of his contemporaries, 'and a compass there would sweep his nose, forehead, and chin within the perimeter.'

For many months Oates led a hand-to-mouth existence during which time he was befriended and helped by a few of London's poor Catholics. He expressed a desire to become a Catholic himself and was received into the Church in March 1677. He then discovered in himself a vocation to the Jesuit priesthood and eventually succeeded in getting himself admitted to the secondary school run by the English Jesuits at St Omer, in Belgium, as a pupil. He lasted there some six months, from December 1677 to June 1678, a twenty-eight-year-old oddity among the schoolboys, before being expelled and sent back to London as unfit even to be considered for the Jesuit novitiate. The night before he left, he was found in the chapel, leaning on the altar in the attitude of the priest at the consecration of the Mass. When asked what he was doing, he replied, 'I am bidding farewell to Jesus Christ.'

That six months in St Omer, combined with his Catholic contacts in London, was all that Oates needed. He sat down and in cold blood fabricated the entire 'Popish Plot'. It was to make his name immortal, and deservedly, for no more monstrous invention has ever bubbled from the mind of man. Unlike discoverers of previous plots, Oates knew a good deal about the English Jesuits, their work, their organisation, their names. He skillfully blended fact and fiction into a long narrative, bristling with people and places and dates, and succeeded in getting the document brought before the King's Privy Council. On 28 September he was summoned to appear before the Council in person and there he re-affirmed all the lies written in his narrative and added a few more in the inspiration of the moment. The Council listened in amazement as he detailed the horrid conspiracy for them. The King was to be murdered and his brother put on the throne. The Protestant religion was to be proscribed and leading Protestants put to death. The Scottish Presbyterians were to be incited to revolt. In Ireland a Popish army of twenty thousand horse and twenty thousand foot was ready to rise in rebellion and a French army would be sent to help them. Immediate and drastic action was needed if England was not to be reduced to a helpless vassal of Rome.

The years spent by Titus Oates in concocting the Popish plot had been years of quiet consolidation for Oliver Plunkett. His diocese, he reported to the Internuncio, was now 'completely at peace, except for two priests who are refractory'. He continued his work of visitation and administered the sacraments of confirmation and ordination. According to the careful lists he kept, he had confirmed 48,655 people up to the outbreak of the persecution of 1673, some in places that had seen no bishop for forty years. Now the crowds presenting themselves for confirmation were smaller and the clerical disputes less frequent. In 1676 he even allowed himself the luxury of a holiday and went to spend a few weeks with his friend, John Brennan, in Waterford.

The only real disturbance during these years happened in the diocese of Kilmore, within the province of Armagh, involving the Vicar-General and some of the clergy, which dragged on from 1676 to 1678. It would be wearisome to describe it, except to say that Oliver was called in and gave his judgment against the Vicar-General, a judgment that was eventually confirmed by Rome. The defeated faction sent the usual stream of complaints and accusations to Rome: Oliver was dictatorial, he favoured the Anglo-Irish at the expense of the native Irish, he used his political influence to have some priests arrested, he was too friendly with the Protestants. Asked by Rome to investigate the charges, John Brennan found that only the last had any truth.

As regards the accusation that the Archbishop of Armagh is giving scandal to Catholics by being over friendly with Protestant ministers, I must say that during all the time I have been in this country, I never hear of any such scandal. If by Protestant ministers they mean ministers of the Protestant Church, it is true that he is friendly with one minister, an official of the so-called primate; but this friendship is greatly to the advantage of his flock, for whenever any lawsuits involving Catholics, especially marriage cases, are brought to the Protestant Episcopal Court, this minister sends them on to Dr Plunkett. I have not heard of his being friendly with any other minister of the Protestant Church.

If by Protestant ministers they mean magistrates and ministers of court, it is true that he is friendly with many of them and they are of great help to him, because it means that they can from their own personal knowledge reject the accusations brought against him through the ill-will of clerics and laymen. Were it not for his friendship with these men, he would probably have been banished long ago from the

Kingdom like the Archbishops of Dublin and Tuam, so great
is the malevolence of these informers.

Brennan may have under-estimated Oliver's friendship with
Protestant ministers: it is clear from other letters that Oliver had
friendly contacts with the Protestant Archbishop of Armagh and
Bishop of Clogher. But the real rub was that Oliver was still a
Palesman, a speaker of English, a bearer of Norman blood, with an
entry to the corridors of power that none of the old Irish could any
longer command. For some of the old Irish this was and always
would be Oliver's unforgivable sin. They did not want this man to
rule over them.

Oliver was now in his early fifties, a fairly advanced age by the
standards of those days. The years of constant travel and hardship
had taken their toll of him, both in body and in spirit; a letter of
1677 speaks of the humiliation of the Irish bishops in their journeys:
'they have to go today to the house of one gentleman for their meals
and tomorrow to another's, which is shameful for the bishops and
wearisome for the gentry'. By August 1678 his eye-trouble had
become quite severe.

> The last two months were spent in making a difficult and
> tiring visitation of my diocese, of which I shall shortly give a
> full account to Your Excellency. . . . The journey through the
> mountains of the northern districts was very fatiguing and it
> made the running from my eyes much worse so that I can
> hardly write or read letters even if they are as large as a snuff-
> box. Still, it did not stop my tongue from preaching both in
> English and in Irish.

He had given everything he had to the service of his God and of his
Church, everything except his life. Now that sacrifice too was to be
asked of him.

In August 1678 no one had heard of the name of Titus Oates. By
the end of September his name was on everybody's lips. The Popish
Plot had been an unbelievable success.

Historians are still trying to explain the frenzy that gripped England for the next three years. It owed something to the strange personality of Oates, whose capacity for spontaneous invention is without parallel in human history. It owed something also to the skilful stage-management of Lord Shaftesbury, who lost no time in taking Oates under his wing and using him for his own ends. It was fuelled by the murder of a London magistrate whose death was at once attributed to the Jesuits, and it was augmented by the drove of perjured witnesses who flocked to share in Oates's glittering spoils. The arch-perjurer himself had been transformed from a penniless vagabond into the most adulated man in the Kingdom, with a royal pension, a suite of rooms in the Palace of Whitehall, and the title 'Saviour of the Nation'.

In London and in many parts of England, Catholic priests and laymen were hunted down and imprisoned. The series of trials began that was to lead to the execution of many completely innocent people and to write the most disgraceful chapter in all the annals of English justice. Corrupt and hectoring judges, packed juries, and a mob of shouting and jeering spectators made any kind of defence impossible. The verdict 'Guilty' was a foregone conclusion and the gallows at Tyburn claimed the lives of some of the best men in England.

The political results were equally gratifying. The King, though he knew he was the ultimate objective of the whole attack, felt himself powerless to deal with the situation; he signed the death warrants of his most loyal supporters and granted pensions and rewards to their false accusers. The King's brother, the Duke of York, was forced to leave England altogether and live in exile in Brussels. The Queen, who knew some of the priest-victims personally and hung their portraits in her room, was accused by the insufferable Oates of plotting to poison her husband.

Only one thing was wanting to the full success of the Plot. None of the victims confessed to the crimes of which they were found guilty. This was a blow to the credibility of Oates and his hirelings and they made every effort to extort a confession from the condemned men, even offering them their lives if they admitted their guilt. It was in vain: without exception, they proclaimed their

innocence with their last breath. It was one of the things that would
eventually turn the tide against the Plot, but not for some time yet.

From Ireland, Oliver Plunkett watched events in England with
anxiety. Ireland now had a new Viceroy, the Duke of Ormond,
replacing the Earl of Essex, who had joined Shaftesbury in opposition
to the King. Ormond, the leading Irish nobleman of the time, had
no love for Catholics; but he knew as did everyone else in Ireland that
the Irish part of the Plot with its Popish army of 40,000 men was
completely without foundation. In addition, he had many links by
blood and marriage with the Plunketts; he was unlikely to take any
action against Oliver of his own free will. But to protect his own
position he had to be seen to take some action. He ordered the arrest
of the Archbishop of Dublin, Peter Talbot, who had recently returned
from exile a dying man, and who had the misfortune of having been
named in Oates's narrative; and he followed this with a new edict of
banishment.

Once again Oliver prepared to go underground, and he wrote
from Dublin to inform the Internuncio of the situation on 27
October 1678.

> The Provincial Council had suggested that I should make a
> visitation of the province, so I began with Meath, the first
> suffragan diocese, and then went on to Clonmacnois. I had
> just finished there when the news came by post that Dr Talbot
> of Dublin had been arrested, and imprisoned in the Castle or
> Tower of this city. I heard this on the 21st of this month.
> Immediately after that a proclamation or edict was issued
> banishing all the archbishops, bishops, vicar-generals, and all
> the regular clergy, ordering them to leave the Kingdom before
> the 20th of November, and threatening fines and penalties
> against anyone found giving them food or drink or helping
> them in any way.
>
> I was quite astonished at the arrest of the Archbishop of
> Dublin, especially as he had not performed any ecclesiastical
> function since his return to Ireland. The houses of the
> unfortunate regulars have been closed and the clergy scattered:

so the edict puts an end to all the disputes and the plans for reform. The parish priests and secular clergy are not included in it. It is not known what exactly the Archbishop of Dublin is being charged with; he is being held in the secret prison and no one can communicate with him.

A number of people have been arrested in London for conspiring against the King, for corresponding secretly with foreign rulers, and for the murder of a nobleman who was found dead in London. As for the plot against the King, it is a complete invention.

I have not been included by name in the present edict, nor was I in the one of four years ago; so I will stay on in the kingdom, but inconspicuously in some country place. Dr Brennan will probably be with me. I heard this morning that Dr Talbot will be sent to London for trial: whatever happens endurance will conquer all adversity.

From now on, be good enough to address your letters thus: 'For Mr Edward Hamon, Dublin'; and I will no longer write to Your Excellency under the name of Monsieur Pruisson, but as Monsieur Picquet à Bruxelles.

How Oliver spent the winter of 1678–79, his second winter as a fugitive, we are not told. He may have been unable to send letters or they may have been intercepted on the way. The next the Internuncio heard of him was a letter of 15 May 1679:

Things here are going from bad to worse. First the prelates and regulars were ordered into exile, now they are turning on the parish priests and several of them have been put in prison. If a fair-minded Protestant shows them any kindness, he is called a Papist by the others, which is regarded as a great insult. Colonel Fitzpatrick, an excellent Catholic though a relative of the Duke of Ormond, was banished from Court, and in London they are trying to bring charges against the Duke of York himself.

A reward has already been offered to spies and constables and soldiers, 40 crowns for the arrest of a prelate and 20 for a regular. I am morally certain of being captured, there are so many hunting for me. But, whatever the danger, I will stay with my flock and will not abandon them until I am dragged to the ship.

However, in case I am captured, I would like you to tell me where I should go; they have given others a choice, I am sure they will do the same to me. Please let me have your advice or recommendation on this, whether I should go to France or Flanders or somewhere else.

10

The Arrest of Mr Meleady

For another six months Oliver enjoyed a precarious liberty. Although he did not know it, he as still being shielded by Ormond's goodwill. It was not until the end of October that Ormond finally issued orders for his arrest at the express command of the Privy Council in London. The Council had been informed that Oliver was involved in a plot to set up a French army for the invasion of Ireland and they wanted him arrested and questioned. Ormond was not prepared to risk his position by dragging his feet any longer and he immediately set his spies on the track of the Primate as a matter of the utmost urgency.

Before long, he had some definite information to go on. Oliver had been seen staying near the Naul, a village a few miles north of Dublin, under the name of Mr Meleady; he had cut off his beard and moustache and was wearing a wig. The wig is not so dramatic as it sounds; it was customary for gentlemen of quality to wear a periwig and to go clean-shaven. Oliver was no longer of an age when he could carry off the role of an army officer; the name Mr Meleady suggests elderly respectability and the disguise went with it. His presence near Dublin was probably explained by the fact that his old friend and tutor Patrick Plunkett was dying, full of years and honour, in the seventy-sixth year of his age.

On 30 November Oliver was still at liberty. On that day he wrote to Rome to inform them that the aged bishop had at last gone to his reward.

> I must give you the sad news of the death of Dr Patrick Plunkett, Bishop of Meath, a prelate distinguished by his birth, his sincerity, his integrity of life, his skill and experience in matters ecclesiastical, and his devotion to his duties as a bishop for thirty-three long years. . . . He died poor because he

lived rich, generous in his alms-giving. His right hand did not know what his left hand was doing. He never denied charity to anyone in need and he gave many gifts in secret to those who were ashamed to let their poverty be known, to respectable men and to widows, of whom we have a large number since the massacre of Cromwell.

On 6 December 1679, Oliver Plunkett was arrested. It is not known how or where, except that it was somewhere in or around Dublin. He was taken to Dublin Castle and there lodged in the secret prison, in the next cell to the Archbishop of Dublin. For six weeks he was held incommunicado in solitary confinement while his papers were examined in vain for something that appeared even remotely treasonable. It was not until 17 January 1680 that he was given the opportunity of writing to Rome and giving some information about his situation.

May the Lord be praised, who has given me two reasons for spiritual rejoicing. The first is my imprisonment in this tower or royal castle, where I was held in strict confinement from 6 December until yesterday, when I was given permission to speak with some friends and my servants; this was because they examined my papers and found nothing about politics or temporal affairs, with which I never concerned myself. The second is the news of the calumnies of an apostate friar, Anthony Daly, bosom friend of Father Felim O'Neill.

The rest of the long letter is a point by point answer to accusations made against him by Daly, the Franciscan friar who had allegedly sent the Tories to assassinate Oliver six years previously. For the last year he had been bombarding officials in Rome and Brussels with allegations about the Primate's misdeeds. Many of the incidents and names he mentioned are as obscure to us as they were to the Roman officials, but some of the charges were manifestly absurd, such as that Oliver had deliberately instigated the recent persecutions in order to rid himself of his enemies. ('This calumniator says that I alone am in favour while others are persecuted,' wrote Oliver. 'How is it then that

I am in prison and they are free?') There is almost a tone of despair about Oliver's letter, as if he had given up hope of ever catching up with the slanders against him. It is saddening and shaming to read his attempts to clear his name with Rome, a prisoner already marked down for death.

At this stage, Oliver probably did not realise the danger he was in. He had broken the law of *Praemunire*, and had resisted the decree of banishment, but the punishment for these offences was not death; he still expected to be deported to some place on the Continent of Europe. It was only gradually that he came to realise that he was being set up as the prime mover of the Irish branch of the Popish Plot and that Shaftesbury and Oates had sent agents to find witnesses against him. They found two among the disaffected clergy of Oliver's own diocese. One was Edmund Murphy, who had been parish priest of Killeavy until suspended from his position by the Primate. The other was John McMoyer, a Franciscan from the Armagh friary, one of the two who had beheaded Oliver's bust in Rome.

During the spring and summer of 1680 Oliver remained in Dublin Castle while the case was being built up against him. His conditions had improved a little. He had a cell with a small balcony on which he was allowed to walk to take the air, and was allowed to have his servant, James McKenna, with him. For these privileges he had to pay £1 a week. His jailers seemed to have been reasonably humane and his friends were allowed to send him in food.

In the next cell, Peter Talbot was slowly dying. Whatever rivalry had existed between the two was forgotten in a dramatic incident that occurred at this time. Dr Mark Forristal, the newly appointed bishop of Kildare, reported it to Rome in a letter of 5 June, written in unusually elegant Latin.

> The unfortunate archbishop of Dublin is suffering from an illness which affects his brain and his whole body and on last Friday the good man very nearly breathed his last. Despite the reluctance of the jailers, the Primate forced his way in to him in order to console him and give him absolution. The Primate himself, in the same prison, is uncertain of his fate and of his future. He is in the strictest confinement because he has been

the subject of false accusations by good-for-nothing ruffians and, shameful to say, treacherous priests, who are trying to revenge themselves on him.

Talbot lingered on for a few more months before death released him from his prison cell. Whether the two archbishops ever met again we are not told.

The Viceroy ordered Oliver's trial to be held in Dundalk towards the end of July. This was greatly to Oliver's advantage, as he was well known to everyone in the area. It was disastrous for his two accusers, who were also well known there as former inmates of the town jail. What followed was described in detail by Oliver in a letter of 25 July.

I was brought under guard to Dundalk on 21 July; Dundalk is about 36 miles from Dublin. I was put into the custody of the King's Lieutenant for that district, who treated me with great courtesy.

On 23 and 24 July I had to appear in court. A long list of charges was read but McMoyer failed to appear on the 24th to confirm his statements and answer my defence. I had thirty-two witnesses, priests, friars and layman, all prepared to refute everything the friar had sworn: namely, that I had seventy thousand Catholics prepared to murder all the Protestants and to establish here the Romish religion and Popish superstition; that I had sent various agents to different kingdoms to obtain aid; that I had visited and explored all the fortresses and maritime ports of the kingdom; and that I had held a provincial council in 1678 to introduce the French. He had also in his sworn statements made accusations against Monsignor Tyrrell, the Reverend Luke Plunkett and Doctor Edward Dromgoole, an eminent preacher.

The other witness, Murphy, fled from the kingdom when he heard that the trial was to be held in Dundalk; McMoyer claimed that he could not come forward himself as he was waiting for Murphy to return; and so the trial ended. According to the law of this country I must attend three assizes before I can be acquitted, and as there will not be another assizes in Dundalk until the end of next March my counsel and friends have advised me to present a petition to have the case heard in Dublin at the next assizes at All Saints and to have the Dundalk jury brought to Dublin. It is possible I may succeed in having this granted to me.

The method of procedure in criminal cases here seems quite extraordinary to me. The defendant knows nothing of the charges against him until the day of his trial, he is not allowed a counsel to defend him, his witnesses cannot take the oath, and one witness is sufficient to make the case for the Crown. The witnesses for the defence, however, are allowed to give evidence but not under oath.

After the sitting I was brought back by the Viceroy's orders to Dublin Castle, to my costly and expensive apartment. But Dundalk was even more expensive, even though I spent such a short time there, because I had to bring thirty-two witnesses from different parts and pay their expenses for four days in Dundalk, and I distributed about 40 crowns among the guards and servants of the Lieutenant.

Although the two chief judges are appointed by the Crown, the Lieutenant of the district of Dundalk chooses the jury. As there are more Catholics than Protestants in the County of Louth, McMoyer knew that there would surely be some Catholics on the jury; he also knew that the Lieutenant, officially called the Sheriff, was a friend of mine; so he presented a petition that no Catholic should be on the jury and this was granted to him. I raised no objection to this, as I knew that all the Protestants of my district looked upon McMoyer as an accomplice of the Tories, for which he was prosecuted and fined at the Armagh sessions in 1678. I also knew that they all regarded the accusations McMoyer made against me as wild inventions. Moreover, his dissolute life was notorious and he was always half drunk when he appeared in court.

The reason why Murphy fled was because he knew full well that the jury in Dundalk would have hanged him. He had been in prison in Dundalk and escaped. He had been found in the company of the Tories and had concealed their stolen goods.

It was only at this abortive trial in Dundalk that Oliver realised what kind of charges were being made against him, charges that carried the death penalty if proved. He knew, however, that no jury in Ireland would find him guilty of such absurdities. Unfortunately, Shaftesbury now realised the same thing and he set to work to have the trial transferred to London. Ormond protested that it was unprecedented and illegal for anyone to be tried in England for a crime committed in Ireland, but Shaftesbury managed to produce one very shaky precedent and Ormond was over-ruled. On 24 October, Oliver was taken from Dublin Castle and put on board ship for England. Five days later he was lodged in Newgate prison in London.

11

THE COURT OF KING'S BENCH

For the next six months, while Oliver remained in solitary confinement, Shaftesbury and Oates worked hard on the Irish plot. The English plot was by now showing signs of wear and tear and some distressing incidents had recently occurred. Among these was the acquittal of one or two of those accused by the Saviour of the Nation, including a distinguished Benedictine priest, Father Maurus Corker. Father Corker was still in prison in Newgate but the fact that he and others were alive at all cast a slur on the reputation of Oates and his allies. A really blood-curdling Irish plot was the best hope for retrieving the situation but witnesses were needed to give evidence of its existence.

There was no shortage of candidates. Ireland had more than its share of criminals in that disturbed period and they began to flock to London in search of reward and, even more important, pardon for past offences. Evil-looking characters in leather jackets and brogues hung around Oates's apartment in Whitehall and Shaftesbury's elegant house in Aldersgate Street. The difficulty was to find someone among them who could tell a coherent story in court. When sober, they could hardly speak comprehensible English; when drunk, as they generally seemed to be, they were incapable of anything beyond uttering rude cries in Erse. Even the repulsive Oates found it difficult to stomach the company of the jailbirds, horse-thieves and highwaymen, and when denouncing his royalist opponents in England he could find no worse term of abuse than to compare them to Irish Tories. By a strange quirk of history the epithet struck, and the English Conservative party is know as the Tory party to this day.

Eventually the list was narrowed down and the successful candidates were rehearsed in their recitations. To McMoyer and Murphy a third priest was added. He was Hugh Duffy, a Franciscan, who had been McMoyer's partner in the Rome escapade and later became Murphy's curate in Killeavy, where his parish duties seemed to include robbery with violence. This trio of desperadoes formed a firm nucleus; with the addition of half a dozen or so supporting players, they were adjudged fit to appear before the Grand Jury, the body that had to decide what cases were to be brought to trial. Their first appearance in February was a disaster and they contradicted one another hopelessly; but a second attempt, after another two months of rehearsal, was more successful. The Grand Jury ordered that the Primate be brought before the Court of King's Bench on 3 May 1681.

From October 1680 until May 1681 Oliver had been kept in solitary confinement in Newgate prison. During that long winter, one of the coldest in living memory, he never saw a friendly face or heard a friendly voice. His faithful servant, James McKenna, accompanied him to London in the hope of being able to attend on him as he had done in Dublin; but when he tried to bring him some clean linen in the prison, he was himself arrested and locked up in another part of the jail. The filth of the prison was indescribable, the food uneatable, and the prisoners had to wear irons on their ankles, joined together by a heavy chain. Oliver's health was failing rapidly, and his hair was almost snow white. Shortly after his arrival he was described in the prison records as being 'very ancient and subject to divers infirmities'. Three months later he was suffering 'by reason of his close confinement, and want of assistance for the distemper of the stone and gravel, which often afflicts him'.

That terrible winter in Newgate was the dark night of the soul for the Archbishop of Armagh. It was his testing time, the purifying fire from which he emerged with a new strength and clarity. In the plan of his life, those months of pain and isolation were the time when he was to reach his full stature, the Gethsemane that prepared him for the climb to Calvary. It was only in his last days on earth, after serving that grim tertianship, that he showed how great a man he was, or how great a man he had become. He showed a deep spirituality that had not been seen before, perhaps because the circumstances were not there to reveal it. But he also showed qualities that suggested that he had reached a new and final stage in his voyaging, a serenity, a transparence, a simplicity, a humility, a renouncing of his own will and a willingness to submit to the will of others, that had not been his before. The fettering of his body was the freeing of his spirit. In that fetid cell, in those days and weeks when he prayed without ceasing and to the rigours of his prison added penances of his own, he came at last to a complete understanding and a complete mastery of himself.

Among Oliver's fellow-prisoners was Father Maurus Corker, found not guilty of treason but still confined. Because of his acquittal, he was allowed more freedom than other prisoners and he soon made it his business to find out everything he could about the imprisoned primate. Afterwards he was to write down his recollections of the martyr, and of this period he wrote:

> After his transportation hither he was, as you know, close confined and secluded from all human conversation save that of his keepers until his arraignment, so that here also I am much in the dark and can only inform you of what I learnt as it were by chance from the mouths of said keepers, viz., that he spent his time in almost continual prayer, that he fasted usually three or four days a week with nothing but bread, that he appeared to them always modestly cheerful without any anguish or concern at his danger or strict confinement, that by his sweet and pious demeanour he attracted an esteem and reverence from those few that came near him.

On 3 May, Oliver made his first appearance before the Court of King's Bench. It was a formal proceeding, for the reading of the charges against the prisoner and the fixing of a date for his trial. The judges decided that the trial should be held on 8 June, a bare five weeks away. The prisoner objected that it was illegal to try anyone in England for a crime supposedly committed in Ireland; his objection was over-ruled. He asked for a longer time than five weeks so that he could bring over his witnesses from Ireland; his request was rejected. The Court also refused to let him have a priest visit him, but agreed

to let him see his servant, James McKenna, only recently released
from jail.

The reunion between the Archbishop and his servant was a brief
one. Almost immediately McKenna, accompanied by a relative of
Oliver's, set out for Ireland in the all but hopeless task of rounding up
the witnesses in the short time permitted them. Everything turned out
against them; contrary winds at Holyhead delayed them, the Dublin
authorities refused to give them copies of the criminal records of the
prosecution witnesses, and held up the issuing of safe-conducts for the
defence witnesses. McKenna went back to London to bring the news;
the Archbishop's witnesses were on the way but there was now no
possibility of their arriving in time for the trial.

The trial of Oliver Plunkett was held in Westminster Hall,
London, on 8 June 1681. All the trappings of justice were lavishly
displayed, only justice itself was lacking. At one end of the great hall
on a raised platform sat the three judges in their gold chains and
scarlet robes, headed by the Lord Chief Justice himself, Sir Francis
Pemberton. There were no less than five counsels for the prosecution,
among them Sir George Jeffreys, who soon after immortalised himself
as Judge Jeffreys of the Bloody Assizes, notorious even in an age of
legal bullies. There was a jury of twelve good men and true,
handpicked by Shaftesbury's agents. There was the people of England
represented by the London mob, who normally hooted and pelted the
defence witnesses in the Popish Plot trials: a pleasure that would be
denied them today, since the defence witnesses had only just landed
in Holyhead. There was the prisoner standing alone, compelled to
conduct his own defence without any foreknowledge of the charges to
be brought against him, without any means even of noting down the
various allegations that he would later be expected to answer.

The account of the day's proceedings was soon afterwards printed
in pamphlet form, as was the custom of the time; but the account was
edited to favour the prosecution and discredit the defence. Even in
that unsatisfactory condition, it still reads as a sad and shabby travesty
of justice, a meaningless parade of the forms of legal process without
the content.

The proceedings opened with another appeal from the prisoner
for time to get his witnesses to London, which met with another

rebuff. Then the prosecution started their case. They would bring witnesses to prove that the prisoner had been appointed Primate by the Pope in order to raise an army in Ireland and overthrow the government, that for this purpose he forced the Irish clergy to raise money and make a census of all able-bodied men in the country, and that he toured the harbours of Ireland to find a suitable landing-place for a French invasion, finally settling on Carlingford in County Louth as the best for the purpose.

Nine witnesses in all appeared for the prosecution. In addition to the three priests from Armagh, five laymen and a Clogher priest had been pressed into service. These were supporting players with little to say beyond vague hearsay rumours of plots and letters and mysterious meetings, and their main function was to build up an atmosphere of conspiracy and intrigue. The hard work of pinning the guilt on the Archbishop of Armagh was to be left to the three principles.

The first of the three to speak was the Franciscan, Hugh Duffy. He performed well for his employers, relating with circumstantial detail how he heard the prisoner engaging in treasonable plotting with the Bishop of Clogher and accompanied him on a reconnoitring trip to Carlingford. He had also seen letters from the prisoner looking for money for the rebel army. He was not disconcerted when the prisoner asked him to produce the letters. 'I could have brought them but thought it needless,' he replied loftily.

Edmund Murphy was a different case. As a secular priest of the diocese of Armagh, he owed most loyalty to the Primate and his treachery was the greatest. He was expected to repeat the story he had learnt off for the Grand Jury, of how Oliver had been appointed Primate by the Pope on condition that he would raise a rebellion in Ireland; but faced with his own conscience and seeing his Archbishop already marked down for death, he could not go through with it and began to mumble and hedge.

Attorney General:
Answer my question: have you ever been with Plunkett in Ireland?

Murphy:
Yes, sir.

Attorney General:
Have you ever heard him own himself Primate of Ireland?

Murphy:
Yes, Titular Primate.

Attorney General:
Under whom did he claim that authority? Under the king or under the pope?

Murphy:
I think he could not be under the king at all.

Attorney General:
Under whom then?

Murphy:
It must be either the king or the pope.

Lord Chief Justice:
Answer me directly, did he claim to be titular head under the pope?

Murphy:
I suppose he did.

Lord Chief Justice:
Was he reputed generally so to be?

Murphy:
Yes, my lord.

Attorney General:
Mr Murphy, remember what you swore before the Grand Jury. Pray recollect yourself whether that be true, and tell all.

Lord Chief Justice:
You are upon your oath, you must speak the truth and the whole truth. You must not mince or conceal anything.

Serjeant Jeffreys:
Did you give in any evidence to the Grand Jury?

Murphy:
Yes, I did.

Serjeant Jeffreys:
Was what you swore before the Grand Jury true, upon your oath?

Murphy:
I can't say but it was.

Serjeant Jeffreys:
Repeat it. Tell my Lord and the jury what it was, and tell the truth.

Murphy:
I have forgot it.

Despite further attempts by the Bench and Counsel to jog his memory. Murphy remained unhelpful. 'It is evident,' said the Lord Chief Justice, 'that the Catholics have been tampering with him.' To which Jeffreys replied, 'I desire he may be committed, my lord, because he hath fenced from the beginning.' Accordingly, Murphy was committed to prison for contempt of court.

Fortunately for the prosecution, John McMoyer was at hand to pick up the pieces after this disaster. He was the most fluent of all the witnesses and he never hesitated as he described totally imaginary conversations with the Primate in Armagh and equally imaginary letters written by him to Rome, none of which were produced. The only awkwardness occurred when Oliver tried to shake the witness's credibility by drawing attention to his criminal past. The Lord Chief Justice himself had to come to McMoyer's rescue. 'Look you, Mr

Plunkett,' he said, 'don't misspend your own time; for the more you trifle in these things, the less time you will have for your defence.' He knew, of course, that attacking the credibility of the prosecution witnesses was the only defence that the prisoner had left to him.

After the closing speeches, the Lord Chief Justice summarised the evidence for the jury. 'I leave it to you', he concluded. 'It is pretty strong evidence. He does not say anything to it, but that his witnesses are not come over.' The jury retired and were back again in a quarter of an hour.

Clerk of the Crown:
Oliver Plunkett, hold up thy hand. How say you, is he guilty of the high treason whereof he stands indicted or not guilty?

Foreman:
Guilty.

Plunkett:
Deo gratias, God be thanked.

The Court rose, the hall emptied, and the prisoner was brought back to his cell in Newgate.

By the custom of the time, a week elapsed between the end of the trial and the passing of the sentence. The penalty for high treason was death and this was the penalty that Oliver faced, unless he were granted a reprieve. The King had the power to reprieve but had never had the courage to exercise it for any of the Popish Plot victims, though he was fully aware of their innocence; there was little chance that he would intervene now, even though he was being subjected to unusual pressure.

The outcome of the Archbishop's trial had caused horror not only in Ireland but all over Europe. The Pope urged the Catholic monarchs to do everything in their power to help him. The ambassadors of Austria, Spain and France were instructed to make representations to the English government. The French ambassador reported that Charles said he was more sorry than he could possibly express to see an innocent man condemned but was afraid to grant a reprieve in the circumstances of the time.

Another and quite unexpected intervention came from the Earl of Essex, the former Irish Viceroy, who was now living in London and had joined Shaftesbury in opposition to the King. He went to Charles to assure him of Oliver's innocence and ask for a pardon. Not surprisingly, the King lost his temper. 'Why did you not attest this at his trial?' he asked angrily. 'It would have done him some good then. I dare not pardon anyone. His blood be upon your head, not mine.'

There was only one way in which Oliver could escape the gallows. None of the Plot victims had confessed to their guilt, even though offered their lives if they did. When Richard Langhorne, the Jesuit's lawyer, had been condemned to death, Shaftesbury himself had gone to Newgate to offer him life and fortune in exchange for a confession; but in vain. Now the same offer was made to Oliver.

It was no spirit of benevolence that prompted it. Shaftesbury was now in serious difficulty. For many thoughtful people, in England as well as abroad, the Plunkett trial had been the last straw. The sordid and cynical farce had convinced them not only of the Archbishop's innocence but of the innocence of all those others who had suffered in the name of the same conspiracy. The whole rickety fabric of lies and perjuries was beginning to fall apart and the revulsion caused by the Archbishop's death would complete its ruin. The only thing that could save it was for Oliver to admit his guilt.

The offer was made and rejected. Nothing now stood between Oliver and the sentence of death.

The prisoner made his third and last appearance before the Court of King's Bench on 15 June. Before the sentence was passed, he had to endure a long lecture from the Lord Chief Justice that began with a vicious attack upon his religion.

Lord Chief Justice:
Look you, Mister Plunkett, you have been here indicted of a very great and heinous crime, the greatest and most heinous of all crimes, and that is, high treason; and truly yours is treason

of the highest nature, it is a treason in truth against God and
your king, and the country where you lived.

You have done as much as you could to dishonour our God
in this case; for the bottom of your treason was your setting up
your false religion, than which there is not anything more
displeasing to God or pernicious to mankind in the world. A
religion that is ten times worse than all the heathenish
superstitions; the most dishonourable and derogatory to God
and his glory of all religions or pretended religions whatsoever,
for it undertakes to dispense with God's laws and to pardon
the breach of them.

After another canter over the now well-trodden ground of the
Irish plot, the Lord Chief Justice ended with the pious hope that the
prisoner, now so near his end, would have the grace to repent of his
false religion before it was too late.

Plunkett:
May it please your lordship to give me leave to speak one word.
If I were a man that had no care of my conscience in this
matter, and did not think of God Almighty or conscience or
heaven or hell, I might have saved my life; for I was offered it
by divers people here, so I would but confess my own guilt and
accuse others. But, my lord, I had rather die ten thousand
deaths than wrongfully accuse anybody; and the time will
come when your lordship will see what these witnesses are that
have come in against me.

I do assure your lordship, if I were a man that had not good
principles, I might easily have saved my life; but I had rather
die ten thousand deaths, than wrongfully to take away one
farthing of any man's goods, one day of his liberty, or one
minute of his life.

Lord Chief Justice:
I am sorry to see you persist in the principles of that religion.

Plunkett:

They are those principles that even God Almighty cannot dispense withal.

Lord Chief Justice:

Well, however, the judgment which we must give you is that which the law says and speaks. And therefore you must go from hence to the place from whence you came, that is, to Newgate; and from thence you shall be drawn through the city of London to Tyburn; there you shall be hanged by the neck but cut down before you are dead, your bowels shall be taken out and burnt before your face, your head shall be cut off, and your body divided into four quarters, to be disposed of as his majesty pleases.

And I pray God to have mercy upon your soul.

A few formalities remained. The Court was graciously pleased to allow the condemned man the company of his servant for his last few days on earth; he could also have visitors, as long as there was a warder present. His request for a priest was ignored.

12

THE MARTYR

The last two weeks of Oliver's life were to prove a period of great happiness and peace. All the cares that had been his daily lot for so many years could now be set aside. He was visited by many of his friends and by some of the leading English Catholics, who came to give comfort but instead received it.

It must have been during this time that the Irish painter, Garret Morphey, drew the sketch of him that has formed the basis of almost all subsequent portraits of the Archbishop. The sketch itself has vanished but several copies still exist of an engraving made from it by the Dutch artist, Van der Vaart. It shows a man who looks older than his fifty-five years, with beard and moustache and shoulder-length white hair. The face is lined and worn but it has an expression of great dignity and strength about it. There is an almost other-worldly quality in the levelled eyes, which look without curiosity upon a world that is no longer of anything more than passing interest.

During these last few days he had the company of his servant and friend, James McKenna, who besides attending on him, also carried letters back and forth between him and his fellow-prisoner, Father Corker. Afterwards Corker described the Archbishop as he then appeared:

> The trial being ended and he condemned, his man had to leave to wait on him alone in his chamber, by whose means we had free intercourse by letters to each other. And now it was I clearly perceived the Spirit of God in him, and those lovely fruits of the Holy Ghost, charity, joy, peace, patience, etc., transparent in his soul. And not only I, but many other Catholics who came to receive his benediction and were eye witnesses (a favour not denied to us) can testify.

There appeared in his words, in his actions, in his very countenance, something so divinely elevated, such a composed mixture of cheerfulness, constancy, courage, love, sweetness and candour, as manifestly denoted the divine goodness had made him fit for a victim and destined him for heaven. None saw or came near him but received new comfort, new fervour, new desires to please, serve and suffer for Christ Jesus, by his very presence.

Among the letters he wrote at this time must have been several to his family. One survives, a letter written in English to Michael Plunkett, a relative of his who was studying in the Irish College, Rome. It survives because Michael left it in the Roman archives to be preserved for posterity. Writing to Michael, Oliver must have remembered his own student days in Rome and that prospect of martyrdom that attracted and repelled him at the same time; now he suddenly realises that death no longer holds any fear for him.

Sentence of death passed against me on 15th, without causing me any fear or depriving me of sleep for a quarter of an hour. I am innocent of all treason as the child born yesterday. As for my character, profession and function, I did own it publicly, and that being also a motive of my death I die most willingly; and being the first among the Irish, I will teach others with the grace of God, by example, not to fear death. But how am I, a poor creature, so stout, seeing that my Redeemer began to fear, to be weary and sad, and that drops of his blood ran down to the ground? I have considered that Christ, by his fears and passions, merited for me to be without fear. . . .

I have recommended you to my friends there, and also my nephews and two nieces. Jemmy and Joseph begun their philosophy and Mickey ended his prosody. Catty and Tomasina and all will be in a sad condition. You know that Ned is simple, and that by Cromwell's people what little land and mortgages he had left him by his father were lost; and I believe my friends there will help my nephews, if you speak to Monsignore.

The letters he wrote to his fellow-prisoner, Father Corker, have also been preserved, and they almost form a diary of those days. The first of them seems to have been written the day after his sentence.

> Dear Sir,
> I am obliged to you for the favour and charity of the £20 and for all your former benevolence, and whereas I cannot in this country remunerate you, with God's grace I hope to be grateful in that kingdom which is properly our country. And truly God gave me, though unworthy of it, that grace to have *fortem animam mortis terrore carentem.**
>
> I have many sins to answer for before the supreme Judge of the high bench where no false witnesses can have audience; but as for the bench yesterday, I am not guilty of any crime there objected to me. I would I could be so clear at the bench of the All-powerful, *ut ut sit.*†
>
> There is one comfort, that he cannot be deceived because he is omniscious, and knows all secrets even of hearts, and cannot deceive because he is all goodness; so that I may be sure of a fair trial and will get time sufficient to call witnesses, nay, the Judge will bring them in a moment if there be need of any.
>
> Your and your comrades' prayers will be powerful advocates at that bench (here none are admitted) for
> Your affectionate friend,
> Oliver Plunkett

Two days later, on 18 June, he wrote about some money that had been received from another benefactor; evidently he was becoming a little overwhelmed by his visitors, as the last sentence shows: 'I am informed the execution will be upon Tuesday; and I long to be out of all affairs, and to have one full day and night to recollect myself.' A day or two later, he has still not completely overcome these distractions: 'Oh, if I could but feel one act of true and lively

---

*   A valiant soul without fear of death
†   However it may be

contrition, I would be well satisfied. I often endeavour, but still I find some earthly thought do obstruct and hinder my good inspiration. . . . The passage is but short, yet 'tis dangerous, from time to eternity. It can never be repassed or reiterated. Your prayers I say I beg and your brethren's.'

On the 23rd, a new, and this time definite, date was set for his execution. 'The Captain sent to me Mr Cooper to tell me that tomorrow sennight the execution will be. Whereas 'tis not upon St John's day, I am glad 'tis to be upon his octave and upon a Friday also. He tells me I will be allowed a priest. I desired it should be you. If it will be a person unknown to me, I intend to discourse but little with him.'

The next day, the Feast of St John the Baptist, brought an unusually long letter. Oliver speaks with pride of the constancy of his brother bishops. 'They might have saved their lives by going overseas, but the Irish prelates are resolved rather to die than to forsake their flocks. Forristal Kildariensis had departed but that I hindered him, for if the captains will fly, 'tis in vain to exhort the single soldiers to stand in battle. . . . By our deaths the number of Catholics will not be diminished but rather augmented, when they see we willingly die and contemn life, which is the only idol of our adversaries.' Then he goes on to reflect on John the Baptist, who was beheaded in spite of his stainless life.

> He had not even venials and suffered prison and death; we have dunghills of mortals and what ought we to suffer? But why should I speak of St John, whereas his Master, who was free from all original, venial and actual sins, suffered cold, frost, hunger, prison, stripes, thorns and the most painful death of the cross for others' sins, which death of the cross compared to that of Tyburn, as I hear the description of it, is but a flea-biting.*
>
> I ought therefore cheerfully desire it, heartily covet it, and joyfully embrace it, it being a sure way, a smooth path by

---

* In his haste, Oliver has put this the wrong way round. He obviously means that Tyburn is but a fleabite compared to the cross.

which I may in a very short time pass from sorrow to joy, from toil to rest, and from a momentary time or duration to never-ending eternity.

If the Archbishop was troubled about his sins, his mind was soon set at rest. A day or so after his letter, Father Corker finally succeeded in gaining admission for a short while to Oliver's cell. They heard one another's confessions, gave and received absolution, and promised each other the support of their prayers. Furthermore, the requisites for Mass were brought to the cell, and Oliver had the happiness of celebrating the Eucharist daily for the last week of his life, including the day of his death.

The last seven days of Oliver's life marked the last stage in his spiritual journey. It has been said that self-will dies a quarter of an hour after we do. During his final week on earth, Oliver, who had given up everything else, now gave that up as well. Looking back on his past life, he must have seen one fault that seemed to run its roots deepest into his character. Sometimes it had taken on the appearance of virtue: steadfastness, determination, single-mindedness. Other times it had showed touchiness, his enemies had called it arrogance or high-handedness.

All his life he had been a fighter. When a thing had to be done, he did it regardless of the cost. When criticised for his actions, he had always answered his critics, point for point. He had never doubted that he was in the right. But even in the right, one can sometimes be wrong. The memory of those pathetic priests, his last accusers, was not easily shaken from his mind. He had disciplined them in the past, and justly; but could there have been a place for mercy that his self-righteousness did not see? Had his hardness helped to bring them to that sad pass? Had he given them some reason to hate him so much?

What thoughts went through Oliver's mind in that last week, after his one and only meeting with his priest-friend, we cannot fully know. We do know that, by a deliberate and conscious decision, he stripped himself completely of self-will and submitted totally to the will of another. That other was Father Maurus Corker.

Most of his remaining communications with Corker concerned his speech from the scaffold. This was a matter of some importance, since it would be printed and widely circulated in London and elsewhere. A friend had written a draft for him but he did not like it because it was 'too sharp against Parliament, Judges and Jury', a comment one would not have expected from him in former times. He then made out his own version, which was shuttled back and forth between the two cells for Corker's suggestions and corrections; all his emendations, which were slight enough, were gratefully accepted.

Corker's description of him during these last few days is memorable.

> After he certainly knew that God Almighty had chosen him to the crown and dignity of martyrdom, he continually studied how to divest himself of himself, and becoming more and more an entire, pleasing and perfect holocaust. To which end, as he gave up his soul with all its faculties to the conduct of God, so for God's sake he resigned the care and disposal of his body to unworthy me, and this in such an absolute manner that he looked upon himself to have no further power or authority over it.
>
> For an instance of this, the day before he suffered, when I sent a barber to trim him, the man asked him if he should leave anything on his upper lip. He answered he knew not how I would have it, and he would do nothing without my order, so that they were forced to send to me before the barber could finish his work.
>
> Another remarkable instance of his strange humility and resignation was that, about an hour before he was carried to execution, being desired to drink a little glass of sack to strengthen his spirits, he answered he was not at his own disposal but mine, and that he must have leave from me before he would either take it or refuse it; whereupon, though I was locked up, yet for his satisfaction his man and the keeper's wife came to my chamber, and then returning back told him I enjoined it, upon which he readily submitted.

The strange incident of the glass of wine shows not only his submission to Corker's will, but his desire to follow his Master's example as closely as possible in his passion. He was evidently thinking of the Gospel account: 'they brought him to the place called Golgotha (which means the place of the skull), and they offered him wine mingled with myrrh; but he did not take it' (Mark 15:22–23).

His last letter to Corker was written on the eve of his death.

Sir,

I do most earnestly recommend myself to your prayers and to the most holy sacrifices of all the noble confessors who are in this prison and to such priests as you are acquainted with; and I hope soon to be able to requite all your and their kindness. Above all I recommend myself to the prayers of the holy families of Mr Sheldon and the Lady Staffords, and in general to all the good Catholics in this city whose faith and charity are great.

I do recommend to you and to them my most faithful servant, James McKenna, who served me these eleven years. Some of the good Catholics who came to see me told me that after my death they would be charitable to him.

I desire that you be pleased to tell all my benefactors that for all eternity I will be mindful of them, and that I will pray for them until they will come where I hope to come soon, and then also will thank them *in conspectu supremi Domini.** They deserve all praise in this and, by God's grace, a crown of glory in the next.

I doubt not but their faith, charity and good works will be efficacious with our Saviour, and that there will soon be an end of this persecution and that *iniquitas multorum mox revelabitur. Fiat voluntas Dei, fiat, fiat.*† And I beseech my Saviour to give all the good Catholics perseverence in their faith and good works and to grant me the grace to be

---

* In the sight of the most high Lord.
† The iniquity of many will soon be revealed. God's will be done.

tomorrow where I may pray for them *non in aenigmate* but
facie ad faciem, etc. ††

And be sure that I am and still will be,

Your obliged friend,

Oliver Plunkett

On the night before his death, the Archbishop went to bed at
eleven o'clock and slept quite soundly until four the next morning,
when he was awakened by McKenna who had slept in the cell with
him. He rose and said his last Mass, with McKenna as his server.
Then he dealt with a few items of unfinished business and scribbled
a couple of last-minute messages for Father Corker; though the word
'scribbled' is not altogether appropriate, for the writing is firm and
clear. Then, as we have seen, he drank a glass of sack and waited for
the summons from the prison governor.

Oliver was to have a companion in his suffering that day. He was
Edward Fitzharris, an unfortunate informer who had misjudged his
perjuries and had been caught in the trap he had set for others. He
had been sentenced to death on the same day as Oliver and then
returned to his prison in the Tower of London.

An execution was an elaborate affair in those days and the
procession to Tyburn was an important part of the spectacle. On that
morning of 1 July, the cavalry and foot-soldiers assembled at the
Tower between eight and nine, while Fitzharris was brought out and
put lying on the sledge, a kind of wooden boat dragged along the
ground by horses. Then the procession formed and moved off
through the crowds in the direction of Newgate.

In Newgate, Oliver was taken from his cell and laid on a second
sledge in the press-yard. When asked by the Lieutenant of the Tower
how the Archbishop had borne himself, the Governor of Newgate is
said to have replied: 'Very well, for when I came to him this morning,
he was newly awake, having slept all night without any disturbance;
and when I told him to prepare for his execution, he received the
message with all quietness of mind, and went to the sledge and

††   Not in darkness but face to face.

unconcerned as if he had been going to a wedding.' The procession re-formed itself around the two condemned men and continued on to Tyburn, a distance of about two miles.

At Tyburn they halted in front of the great gallows, where twenty men could hang at a time. Fitzharris, terrified, had to be helped to the gallows, where he retracted everything he had said at his trial and accused Shaftesbury's agents of having suborned him. The Archbishop, by contrast, was perfectly calm as he delivered his prepared speech to the attentive and unexpectedly sympathetic crowd.

He began by detailing the charges that had been made against him under seven heads, and answered each one separately, before going on to a general protestation of his innocence and of the absurdity of the charges to anyone who knew the Irish situation. 'I dare mention farther and affirm, that if these points of seventy thousand men, etc., had been sworn before any Protestant jury in Ireland and had been even acknowledged by me at the bar, they would not believe me, no more than if it had been deposed and confessed by me that I had flown in the air from Dublin to Holyhead.'

He then went on to speak of the false witnesses and particularly of the four priests who had testified against him, 'which wicked act, being a defect of persons, ought not to reflect on the Order of St Francis or on the Roman Catholic clergy, it being well known that there was a Judas among the twelve apostles and a wicked man, called Nicholas, amongst the seven deacons.'

I do heartily forgive them, and also the judges, who by denying me sufficient time to bring my records and witnesses from Ireland did expose my life to evident danger. I do also forgive all those who had a hand in bringing me from Ireland to be tried here, where it was morally impossible for me to have a fair trial. I do finally forgive all who did concur directly or indirectly to take away my life; and I ask forgiveness of all those whom I ever offended by thought, word or deed. I beseech the All-powerful that his divine majesty grant the King, the Queen, and the Duke of York, and all the royal family, health, long life and all prosperity in this world, and in the next everlasting felicity.

Now that I have show sufficiently, as I think, how innocent I am of any plot or conspiracy, I would I were able with the like truth to clear myself of high crimes committed against the divine majesty's commandments, often transgressed by me, for which I am sorry with all my heart; and if I should or could live a thousand years I have a firm resolution and a strong purpose by your grace, O my God, never to offend you. And I beseech your divine majesty, by the merits of Christ and by the intercession of his Blessed Mother and all the holy angels and saints, to forgive me my sins and to grant my soul eternal rest.

Having finished his speech, the Archbishop stood quietly reciting some prayers in Latin while the hangman adjusted the nooses around his neck and the neck of his companion and pulled woollen caps down over their faces. The platform on which they were standing was a cart, drawn by a horse. Three priests hidden in the crowd pronounced the words of absolution as the horse was driven forward and the two men were left dangling from the high gallows beam.

Nearby was the quartering block, with knives and cleavers for the dismembering. Since the hangman was accustomed to use his victims in accordance with the sympathy or otherwise of the crowd, it is likely that the Archbishop was unconscious and perhaps even dead when he was cut down and the butchering began.

A report sent to Rome shortly after his death, probably by an English Jesuit, made this comment:

> All write with one accord that this innocent victim has done and yet performs great good in England, not only by the edification that he gave to the Catholics, but moreover by the change of ideas and sentiments that he occasioned in many Protestants, who now commence to regard all these conspiracies as malicious fictions; and there are great grounds for believing that the fruit which England will derive from his blood will not end here.

The prophecy was quickly shown to be true. The 1st of July was the day when the people of England finally turned against the Popish Plot and its makers. Next morning the Earl of Shaftesbury was arrested and lodged in the Tower of London. Oliver Plunkett was the last man to be martyred for the Catholic faith in England.

13

THE SAINT

The news of Oliver Plunkett's appointment as Archbishop of Armagh did not meet with universal approval among his fellow-countrymen; neither did the news of his canonisation. For three hundred years he has continued to be a controversial figure in Irish history.

There is a saying, popular in Ireland, to the effect that there is no smoke without a fire. On that principle, many people have felt that there must have been some fundamental flaw in the Archbishop's character to have drawn so much obloquy, some sinister secret still under wraps in the inmost recesses of the Vatican archives. Yet there is another saying that may be more apposite, namely, that if you throw enough mud, some of it is bound to stick. The fact that his reputation remains vaguely tarnished to this day may be attributable to the vigour and persistence of the mud-slingers rather than to the accuracy of their aim.

When a man is declared a saint, it does not mean that all his actions have been canonised. There are some saints who seem always to have been saints, from the cradle to the grave. There are others who become saints by sudden act of conversion, turning from a life of sin to a life of holiness. And there are others again who achieved sainthood by a lifelong process of growth, grace building upon nature, which only reached its fullness with the end of life itself. St Peter, most unrocklike of rocks, was one of those. Oliver Plunkett was another.

It is not that he was ever anything less than a good man, a devout priest, and a holy archbishop. When we examine the accusations against him, they are hard to substantiate. The allegations of unchastity boil down to the two months' career of Captain Brown, an episode that a modern generation finds endearing rather than shocking. The Oliver of the singing pubs may never make the stained-glass windows, but he shows a humanity and enterprise that disarms criticism.

The charge that he showed a certain lack of courage when he chose Rome in preference to Ireland may have a little more basis in fact. At the same time, an excessive desire for martyrdom is unhealthy: it is something to be accepted when offered, not something to be sought. It is true that he stayed in Rome when persecution raged and returned when it had stopped, but it is equally true that he stayed on in Ireland when the persecution was renewed and when he might have chosen exile without too much dishonour. It is impossible to underestimate the importance of that decision for the Irish Church in an age when absentee bishops were common even in the peaceful countries of Southern Europe. By word and example he hammered home the principle that a bishop's place was with his people, that a bishopric was a service to be rendered rather than a benefice to be enjoyed, that it was sheer hypocrisy to exhort the private soldiers to stand if the captains fled. If that was something that later generations in Ireland came to take for granted, it was only because he upheld it at the cost of his life.

The most serious accusation against him and the one that has persisted longest is that he was high-handed and autocratic in his dealings with his clergy. We have already seen how John Brennan found him touchy and hot-tempered in his dispute with the Archbishop of Dublin in 1672. In his great philippic of 1679 Friar Anthony Daly went a good deal further. 'The Primate, acting in a manner that can only be called Machiavellian, seems to think that he cannot rule his subjects properly unless he divides them into factions and then treats these with alternate favour and disfavour. . . . There is no diocese in Ulster that he has not deprived of its Vicar-Generals, scarcely any parish where he has not deposed the parish priest to the scandal of the clergy and the people.' Allowing for the hyperbole, it is still true that Oliver's relations with the clergy were often stormy and acrimonious and that he felt called upon to use his powers of suspension and deposition with some regularity.

Was he a Counter-Reformation bigot and bully, ready to fire all his artillery at the first hint of disobedience? Or did he find himself faced with a critical situation that could only be dealt with by the most drastic measures? The evidence suggests that the second reading is the truer one, that discipline among the clergy had broken down to such an extent that the very existence of the Church was threatened. The collapse of the Catholic Church in England around this period is attributed by historians to the fact that there were no resident bishops to give firm leadership and put an end to the constant squabbling among the clergy.

Whether Oliver acted justly in individual instances can be judged only be examining the individual instances; and in most cases it is no longer possible to do so. We know there were times when he treated delinquent priests with great kindness, among them the Franciscans Harold and Coppinger and the Augustinian French. In other cases he acted more harshly, with what justification we cannot now judge. The clergy have their rights, but so have the laity. When the local parish priest is supporting himself and his houseful of illegitimate children by means of highway robbery, something more than a disapproving silence is called for. If his way of acting was autocratic, it may also have been necessary; and it was certainly courageous, for he knew well the risks he was running in tangling with some of these men.

Finis coronat opus, as Oliver with his liking for Latin tags might well have remarked: the ending crowns the work. For him it proved to be a long-drawn-out ending: almost a year in Dublin Castle, another eight months in Newgate, of which six were spent in solitary confinement, before the final ordeal. For at least twelve of those nineteen months he lived in the constant expectation of a cruel and violent death.

That imprisonment and especially that extraordinary half year in the solitary cell, when in the cold and darkness of winter he fasted even from the scanty prison food for three days a week and spent his time in continuous prayer, was his greatest test and his greatest victory. All that was good in him was strengthened and intensified, all that was unruly was brought into obedience. His will was led to that perfect conformity with the will of God, which is the essence of sainthood.

Without those last nineteen months we might remember him as a devoted and courageous churchman and nothing more. But those months were as much a part of his life as anything that went before; in the divine plan, they were the time given him for the final perfecting of his great soul. The noose that closed around his neck at Tyburn made him a martyr. The life that had prepared him for that noose had already made him a saint.

NOTES AND ACKNOWLEDGEMENTS

The eagerly awaited edition of Oliver Plunkett's letters by Mgr John Hanly was regrettably not yet available at the time when this book was written. The text of the Roman letters is therefore mainly from the versions given in Cardinal Moran's *Memoir of Oliver Plunkett*, though the translation has been modernised. The English letters are taken from the printed versions given in *The Downside Review of 1921*, but with spelling and punctuation brought up to day. The text of the Irish verses is taken from *Dánfhocail*, edited by Thomas F. O'Rahilly.

A special word of acknowledgment is due to Father Tomás Ó Fiaich and Father Benignus Millet, O.F.M., for their generous assistance and for providing some quotations that do not appear to have been published before, notably those on pages 45 and 59.

In the seventeenth century, England and Ireland used the Old Style Calendar, which was ten days behind that used in most other parts of Europe. Thus the date of Oliver Plunkett's death, the first of July, corresponds to the eleventh of July in modern reckoning.